Each Time My Eyes Open

By Marie Maloney

ISBN:1477442820
ISBN-13:139781477442821

DEDICATION

This book is dedicated to the people that have been there for me over the years. I love you all dearly.

PREFACE

Give every man thine ear, but few thy voice;

Take each man's censure,

But reserve thy judgement.

(William Shakespeare, Hamlet I, iii, 65)

CONTENTS

FOREWORD

It all began in my early teenage years when I was still learning about the world and how to trust people. I had only had a few boyfriends, but nothing serious, until I met somebody who I thought was the best thing in the world. He was the one who introduced me to heroin. Unfortunately, I had to learn the hard way, that this was the first step on the road to trouble and misery. I was completely unaware that my problems were escalating beyond my control until I woke up one day feeling as though I had the flu, but a hundred times worse. It was only then that I realised I had made a huge mistake. This wasn't a mistake I could easily change, but one that was to steal many years of my life to come.

Each time my eyes open when I wake up, the first thing that enters my head is the deadly drug, heroin. My day entails having to buy my drugs before I can actually do anything else. I have no energy and feel incredibly ill. My whole day depends on taking a drug before I can even begin to function normally. It is just like 'Groundhog Day'; a reoccurring event that I have to live through every day. I have absolutely no control over this repetitive nightmare, which drives me mad and makes me so unhappy. It has completely ruled and ruined my life, and the lives of thousands of other people in the world, who are in exactly the same situation as me.

There is a common belief amongst addicts that you stop at the age you begin taking heroin and you don't actually grow up like normal people. I certainly feel that I was robbed of those years of normal development. I didn't have the chance to adapt and become the woman I am today. I have missed so much through the years of addiction, which I hugely regret. I was so venerable and naive when I first started taking the drug. At that age, I still had no idea about the world around me, and how dangerous it could be. Even now, I sometimes feel that I am still that fourteen-year-old girl that started using heroin all those years ago.

We all have choices, but unfortunately drug addiction isn't something that you can just change with a click of your fingers, or with a magic wand. People say, why don't you stop? I have done many times, but it's extremely hard coming off heroin, and it is a thousand times harder staying off. It's like a naughty voice in the mind telling you to have some more and you just cant get it out of you head, and it persists for many years.

This book is about my journey, which I want to share with the world. Nobody is perfect, that's what makes us human, and it is true that we can be extremely destructive at times without realising. Despite my addiction I have tried to be like any other normal human being, longing to achieve my goals and dreams.

I have now forgiven people for leading me down the wrong path at a time when I was gullible and easily influenced, but I won't ever forget what transpired. We can't blame others for our own mistakes, but sometimes the fault is not entirely of our own making; others often have a huge influence on us, and can drag us down with them. Fortunately, over the years I've leant to surround myself with positive people and that's what makes a huge difference in moving forward.

This is a true story. Some of the names and places have been changed to protect the identity of the people involved.

MOVING HOUSE

I was born into a loving family: my mum and dad and two older sisters. We lived in a cottage called the Hollow in a little village called Stanstone. I was so young I don't really remember much at this point as we only lived there until I was three years old. My mum told me I was a great baby, but she often worried about how much I slept. I was a rather chubby looking baby as I loved my food and would sleep more than most babies. My mum gave all us children a soft cover, which we all named our 'fuffers'. Years later my mum told me she could only wash my fuffer when I was asleep. I would sit and rub it on the end of my nose until I fell asleep. I think it was a comfort stage I went through until I was a toddler.

We moved to the next village after a few years. I was five years old when my mum, my sisters and I moved into our new house. I remember the day quite clearly even though I was still only very young. It's funny how only certain things stay with you and its usually things that are horrific, sad or extremely good moments in life. My mum told us that she was leaving my dad in a way that a five year old could understand. Things weren't really working out between them. I didn't really understand, but what child would, at that age. I know this happens to thousands of couples everyday, and our family was just one of them. I was so young I didn't really understand the situation and it didn't make any big life changes to me at that age.

We were leaving a four-bedroom house and going into a three-bedroom semi-detached the other side of town, about five minutes drive away. As we arrived at our new house, I remember feeling a mixture of different emotions. I had left all my friends that I had made in the couple of years of living at our original family home. They were also my friends that I went to school with, so I would still get to see them everyday. I also noticed how my sisters were reacting to this new change in our lives, and I could see that they were feeling a little apprehensive. At least, that's what I thought at the time.

We all walked up the long driveway to our new front door, which was quite an old-looking white wooden door. My mum opened it and we went into a very cold and bare living room. It was the complete opposite of the house we had just left. My first impressions were that it looked really old inside, and when I mean old, I mean it needed some attention. It didn't feel homely at all and I could see by my sisters' faces that they were also a little disappointed. Looking back, my mum had done her best to make a fresh start for all of us, and I think it was really brave of her to start over again from nothing, as a single mother with three children. It's something I will always cherish and admire about her.

The outside of the house didn't look too bad, but it hadn't been redecorated in years, because an old couple had lived there before us. Later that evening after settling in a bit, my mum asked me to get ready for bed, and to put my nightie on. I then went down to the living room, where there was no carpet at all, which made it seem very cold and uninviting. The living room and dining room were all in one, so it was quite a long room. There was an old gas fire in the living room that my mum put on because she wanted the house to warm up a bit. I sat quite close to the fire, watching the television as my mum pottered around trying to put all our things into the rooms where they belonged, and getting our school uniforms ready and pressed for the next day. I vividly remember just sitting there, warming myself by the fire, and the next thing I knew my nightie almost caught fire because I was so close. Luckily, my mum just walked in and noticed what had happened, and pulled my clothes off in a panic. It was a lucky escape, and not the sort of thing you need on the day you first move into a new house.

Later on my mum told me to go to bed, and I remember lying there, and not being able to sleep, because I needed to get accustomed to my new surroundings. I felt scared and unsettled. I had all my teddy bears around me, which I cuddled close to my face, because I didn't want to look around the dark room. I was thinking that there was probably something nasty watching me. Eventually I finally found the courage to slip out of bed, and wandered into my mum's room to ask her if I could sleep with her. I felt much better knowing I had my mum there with me, making me feel much safer. My mum had some scary china dolls in her room that I never liked because, I always felt as though their eyes were watching me. Anyway I snuggled into my mum and soon drifted into a deep sleep.

After a few weeks, things began to feel much more homely. My sisters had made their room look nice, and mum was much happier knowing that she was coping with making a fresh start. It didn't take long before my mum got the house organised and looking homely. My mum is a lady who wanted everything just right: no dust on anything and not a crumb on the floor. She would follow us kids, and pick bits from the carpet on her hands and knees. The house was always spotless.

It wasn't long after we moved into our new home that my eldest sister decided she wanted her own room and privacy, so we exchanged rooms and I shared the biggest room with my sister Karla. I had never before had such a big bedroom, so I quite enjoyed the change. My mum brought some little bedside lights which meant that I could read my favourite books at night, which I loved doing. One of my favourite books was 'The Lion, the Witch and the Wardrobe'. I was also a great lover of Roald Dahl books. Reading was something I loved, as I could imagine I was one of the characters in the story. I had an extremely imaginative mind and reading would keep me occupied for hours.

GOLDIE

The only pet I had during the time we lived at our old house was a goldfish, but I remember that particular pet very clearly. I sat on my bed, in my old bedroom, which was painted white, with a 'My Little Pony' border around it. I sat chatting to my goldfish, (I think its name was Goldie). At the time I thought of Goldie as another toy that I could play with, like my Barbie doll. I would talk to Goldie and make up my own stories with Goldie as one of the characters. I remember walking to the small toilet in the house, and taking quite a large bit of toilet paper back to my bedroom. I put my hand into the goldfish bowl to grab Goldie, who swished around trying to escape my clutches. I finally got hold of him, and wrapped him in the toilet paper before putting him on the bedside table. I was convinced that I'd made him feel much better because he was no longer feeling cold. Time passed by and I started to wonder why Goldie was no longer moving. I ran to my mum and showed her Goldie lying so still in my tiny hand. I remember my mum asking me what had happened? I explained Goldie just needed to be warm up a bit.

Mum smiled back and explained that you can't take fish out of water because they can't breath unless they are under water. I looked at her with barely any understanding of what I'd actually done. My mum was extremely careful about the whole thing and without upsetting me she told me that Goldie had gone to heaven. At that point we said a small prayer and flushed him away. I still remember it so clearly, I must have had an over active imagination.

I loved animals and I pestered my mum for ages, ever since we moved into our new house, if we could get a dog. My sisters also wanted a pet because we weren't allowed any big animals when we lived with dad. Eventually, my mum decided to drive us all to a kennels that sold pedigree dogs so that we could take a look at some different breeds, and hopefully take one home with us. We finally arrived at the destination and got out of the car and walked along a stony driveway, until we came to a large building. I could hear all the dogs barking as we walked into an office to give our name. A quite chubby lady stood behind the counter chatting on the phone, but once she saw us waiting she turned around to help.

The lady came across as very helpful, and she took us into the kennels where there were a number of dogs. We were so excited at seeing all these different, lovely looking pups. There were so many to choose from, but my mum had her heart set on a King Charles spaniel or a Yorkshire terrier or even both. The owners kept them in little sheds, which were obviously heated. The first one we came to was where the King Charles spaniels were kept. They were all curled up together on a dog bed with lots of blankets, and when they saw us they all jumped up and plodded over to us with their big paws.

We had our eyes on one spaniel that was slightly different to the rest because he had different markings. We then went along to the next lot of puppies, which were very cute Yorkshire terriers. We spotted another gorgeous puppy, which was smaller than the rest of that particular litter. It was so difficult to choose between the two pups. Mum eventually decided on having them both. At least they would both have the company of each other. On the way home we were all trying to think of names for them and we all finally decided on calling them Charlie and Pudding. They were so adorable that we all fell in love with them once we got them home. It felt so right, at that time, and I remember being a very happy and normal seven-year-old little girl.

I made lots of friends over the period that we lived in our new street. We had lots of fields surrounding our house, and a brook that ran along the whole side of the field. Our street had been an orchard many years before, which is why there were still lots of fields surrounding our housing estate. The two principal streets were even named Cherry Lane and Orchard Terrace. We would walk down to the fields most days, and also down to the brook with our two dogs. It was such a great walk in the summer. The brook ran down the side of a cornfield, which was at least a mile long. It was great fun because it had small hills that we could walk down to get to the brook. We had the option of walking along the field or down beneath the trees where the brook was. It was extremely steep getting down to the brook, but as a child it made it a lot of fun. I had many great times as a kid playing and paddling in that brook, I did what any other child would do; I played and had fun.

PRIMA DONNA

I remember one day when my mum took me shopping in the next town, where my Nan lived. We drove round and round the multi-story car park trying to find a space and eventually she found one right at the top. I held my mum's hand tightly as we walked towards the elevator down to the shopping centre level. I always stood on the big weighing scales that were located just outside the lift. Compared to me the scales looked like a giant. I'd stand and look up at them each and every time we went shopping.

There was also something else that I loved when I went shopping with my mum. There was a large carved wooden dragon for children to play on, and this always made shopping day an adventure. One time, after my mum had finished shopping and talking to so many people she knew or bumped into, I was impatient to go home. As we walked past Boots, the pharmacy, and I noticed people taking pictures of children, because I could see there were flashing of lights coming from the shop entrance.

I pleaded with my mum to have my photo taken too. I was extremely persistent and a very determined young girl, and when I had my mind set on something, it happened. My mum refused at first because I hadn't got my best clothes on, and I had chocolate down my top.

Like I said I was persistent: there was no stopping me. Ever since I can remember I have always enjoyed having my picture taken. A friend of my dad often called me a 'prima donna'. I had no idea what it meant, but I suspected it was something to do with showing off in front of a camera. Anyway, I pulled my mum's hand and went over to the photographer who was taking the pictures.

He told us that they were running a 'baby and children' competition. The winner would get £100 pounds, some clothes vouchers, and the parents would get a bottle of champagne. The winning photo would also appear in the local paper.

Mum decided to let me have my photo taken, and tucked my blue t-shirt into the little red summer skirt that I was wearing, to try to make me look as neat and presentable as possible. I also had a very neat and tidy hairstyle at the time. A short while earlier I had beautiful curls, but after an incident with some chewing gum, I had to have my hair cut.

The photographer then asked me to sit on a chair with my hands together on my lap, and then give him the biggest smile I could manage. I smiled and the pictures were all taken within a few minutes. Afterwards my mum filled in a form with our details on. I was so excited when we left, as I skipped along holding my mums hand. My mum told me not to get my hopes up because there were lots of other children entering the competition.

I was mostly excited that my photo might appear in the newspaper. I don't think I really saw it as a competition; I just loved having my picture taken.

Several weeks went by, and then eventually my mum called me down to the living room to explain that I was in the newspaper and that I had won. My mum was so proud, and the picture turned out to be really lovely.

We accepted the prize and my mum took me to get some new clothes. We had a lovely day out shopping, and it made it much more fun to be able to get some lovely clothes of my choice.

About a week later my mum came back from work, and called me downstairs. I couldn't understand why she sounded so excited. She told me she had a surprise for me. The photographer liked my picture so much that he decided to blow up my photo and put it in the front of his shop window. She had walked past it on her dinner break, so she decided to go inside to find out if she could buy it. At that point she pulled the picture from behind the settee.

It was as big a surprise for me too. The photo was in a posh gold frame and I loved it. My mum put a nail in the wall and hung my picture for all to see. For me, this was my first achievement and it felt really good.
I usually visited my dad on a Friday and we would often go and get either sausage and chips or kebab to eat. It was our little private routine. Afterwards we would get a video of my choice. Dad would tell me to have a bath after eating our meal, and then we would snuggle up on the settee to watch whatever film I had chosen.

Dad was quite strict with all of us. I think mainly because of the way he had been brought up himself, and also because he had been in the Navy. My dad was living in a terraced house only five minutes away from where I lived with my mum and sisters. He had 'on-off' girlfriends, but nothing serious. My dad had done a good job of making his house quite homely, despite being a male on his own, but there were still things that needed doing at that point.

MY PERFECT NAN

My mum and dad met each other in the Navy, and lived together in Singapore before they got married. I think that their time in Singapore must have been the best days for both of them.

I loved my dad, as a youngster, but he wasn't as soft as mum, and sometimes I preferred stopping at home with her, in our new home. When I stayed with my dad, he would often take me to the pub for a quick drink after he finished work. The pub owners knew us very well, so they didn't mind me coming in for a soft drink. My dad taught me to play pool, and I recall that he would constantly remind me to slow down and take my time. Even now, I still have a tendency to rush things.

I also spent a lot of time with my Nan, who I loved dearly. She was what you would call the perfect Nan. My mum worked a lot at the time, so I would go and stay with Nan. She only lived a couple of towns away. On the other hand, my dad's mother lived in London, so we didn't get to see her quite so much, although I did stay with her on a couple of occasions.

Edna Johnson, was my mum's mother, and she lived in a block of flats that had a big field at the side. If you walked across the field you came to a little brook with a small bridge, and further up there was a small play area with swings and a slide. On the other side of the play area there was an indoor swimming pool that she would take us to from time to time.

Across the road from my Nan's flat there was a Catholic school and church. My Nan was a Catholic and she would often take us there on a Sunday. My Nan had a lot of friends who lived in the other flats, and we would often visit them when I stayed with Nan. They were all so nice and they all knew me.

My Nan was great with children, but unfortunately she couldn't have children herself so that's why she decided to adopt my mum and my uncle Pete when they were only babies. Peter wasn't my mum's real brother though. He came from another family.

It's really strange how things work out, because my mum's brother was a very intelligent man. Eventually he got married and had two children of his own. For a time life was great for him, until he and his wife got divorced, which seriously damaged his mental health. He had a nervous break down and then he began to hear voices. He was diagnosed as schizophrenic and it changed his whole way of living and his personality. It was a real shame. We haven't seen him in about five years or more. He just disappeared and hasn't kept in contact. I suppose that's his choice. None of us gets to choose the family we are born into.

When my Nan was a young lady, she wanted to go into the church to become a nun, but she met my granddad first. She decided to go and work in one of the schools serving the food as her job, which she did for several years. Anyway, her love for children was always there throughout her life. She was also the best nurse in the world, and when any of us was sick, she would always be there to comforting us and rub our backs. Children naturally respond to kindness and compassion and that's why I loved staying with her so much. I'd even tell a few white lies sometimes and say I was ill, so I could have the day off to spend with my Nan. She made the best cups of tea, and her honey on toast was sublime. Only Nan could make tea and toast like that.

It must be obvious that my Nan meant the world to me. She was such a good person, and my Nan really looked after us all when we spent time with her. I always felt so safe and contented in her company. I knew that when I wasn't feeling well, that she would make sure that I had everything I needed. Our guardian angel would always be there to nurse all of us. I think her loving nature made us all so close. She was the best we could of asked for.

Where my Nan lived was so peaceful, and the other elderly people were all so nice and polite. Close to my Nan's flat was a small orchard, which blossomed in the spring. I remember that it looked like a fairyland, and I would make up stories as I walked along the narrow track with blossom falling from the trees. I also had a few friends to play with, because other children came to visit their Nans too, and we would build tents outside the front of my Nan's flat, using her clotheshorse. That's why I liked spending time around my Nan's place so much.

MUM'S NEW BOYFRIEND

My family has always been a small one in terms of a family tree, because my mum was adopted from a baby but she never got to find her real mother or father. Some time after we were all settled in our new house, my mum started going out a little to try to find happiness again. She soon met a guy and before we all knew it, he moved in. It was nice to see mum looking happy again. We all knew that mum needed this and we were happy in ourselves to see mum having fun and moving on with life, even though I remember it still felt pretty strange at first.

Adam would take us out in his Land Rover, off-roading, because this is what he liked doing for fun. He was in a local group of Land Rover owners and this was his hobby. He also liked shooting, so we would go clay pigeon shooting at the weekend. After a few months of Adam living with us, I really started looking at him like a stepfather, and became really close to him very quickly. I really needed a father figure in our home and he was doing a good job of this at first.

I was slowly getting accustomed to seeing my mum with a new man. There was a new feeling to the house now that Adam was about, and my mum was smiling again. I could see that they really loved each other to bits. Adam worked as a mechanic and was extremely good with engines for cars. He would be out in the daytime at work and come home around 6pm every evening. At first Adam made a big effort to look good for my mum, despite the fact that he looked like a bit of a biker, to be honest. He had a short black beard, a bit of a chubby rounded beer belly, and an earring that had a gun dangling on the end with a matching necklace. Like I say, he was hugely into his Land Rovers, guns, pubs and beer.

Adam knew that I loved animals, so he planned for us to go to his uncle's place in Swindean. I was so was excited about going I couldn't sit still on our way there to the big farm, where we would be a staying. My mum and Adam told me that there were lots of different animals on the farm; pigs, chickens, horses and goats. The journey was long, but then again any journey for a six year old is long. Needless to say we had to stop off quite a few times for the toilet. I looked out of the window and could see that there were lots of hills and greenery. Eventually Adam told me that we were very close and I could see people on horses riding through the streets. We pulled up to a large gate, which was opened by and a somewhat overweight lady with auburn hair, rosy red cheeks, and a huge smile. I could hear that she had a different accent by the way she greeted us.

As we walked in, another lady introduce herself to me, as Adam's Aunt Steph. She was small with short grey hair and she gave me a big cuddle. I also had the same greeting from Adam's Uncle Ian and their daughter Helen. Adams uncle was a really funny chap; he was slightly deaf so when I spoke to him on a few occasions I had to repeat myself. He asked if I liked horses, and I told him that I loved them. I also added that I would love one of my own. He misunderstood what I said and thought that I did actually own a horse. Adam had to shout that I didn't have one of my own. Uncle Ian also kept on calling me Marilyn by mistake. He was a really eccentric man and a very keen farmer, but made us all feel very welcome. I felt almost like I had been to this place before and I was completely in my comfort zone. I really loved the smell of the farm, the hay and all of the animals. It was such a nice feeling staying there. The country life made me feel like I was at home straight away.

Later I walked around the farm, where I got to stroke lots of different animals and Uncle Ian told me I could walk around with him the next morning to collect the eggs. I found the whole experience fascinating, and couldn't wait for the next morning to bring back breakfast. I was told that I had to be careful of the very large pig they had on their farm because it was slightly dangerous. It wasn't until the next day, as I stood on the gate looking over at all the animals, that this large pig pulled itself over the gate and began to run towards me. I screamed in fright, and at that point Aunt Steph came out and had to smack the pig with a big broom. I was mortified that this pig was so nasty and angry, I couldn't understand why? It was as though it was possessed.

That wasn't the only incident I had whilst we were at the farm. They also had a large turkey, which decided to chase me around the yard. Even though I loved being on the farm, I was a little nervous about walking around on my own. Uncle Ian took me into his barn where he had his wedding coaches, and I imagined the pretty bride sitting up there with her husband to be. They were so grand, and I remember looking at this great big blue cart because it looked so heavy that I felt slightly sorry for the horse or horses that had to pull it. He had big 'shire' horses that pulled these carts and he told me all about how he made all the carts himself. I really found it all very interesting and asked if I could go on it next time I visited them and he agreed.

The next time we visited them they were running the town show, which was called Crickstead Show. I was really excited about this because I would get to see all the horse's show jumping, and the wedding carts being judged. I would also get a chance to sit on some of the big horses. On this occasion my Nan, myself, my two sisters, my mum and Adam was visiting. I recall having a ride in one of the wedding traps. I also vividly remember that it was a gorgeous day, with a red and orange sky as the sun began to set as we pulled into the stables. We also went along to the show the following day as they were holding it in a big field down the road. When I arrived I was really excited. There were people and horses everywhere, and I remember my mum holding on to my hand very tightly. My eldest sister had asked if she could take part in one of the competitions with one of their ponies. It had been made to look the part, with a shiny coat and all its gear on. Once again it was an extremely hot day. I got to sit on a big horse belonging to a friend of Uncle Ian. I had really hoped for an opportunity to ride a horse ever since I first arrived at Swindean.

Just after that I had to run to one of the mobile toilets because I was bursting. My mum wasn't to far away from where I had to go, and she reminded me to come straight back and not to wonder off anywhere.

I ran to the toilet and just as I got there I noticed that there was a black Labrador dog tied up to a post next to the toilets. I really didn't pay any attention to the dog as I was bursting for the toilet and could only think of that. As I ran past this dog, to my surprise, it attacked my leg and it was so fast and unexpected that I ran back to my mum as quickly as I could to show her what had happened. No body else seemed to notice what it had done, so I just had to be brave. The owner of the dog was nowhere to be seen, and I didn't want to hang about to find them. I was slightly in shock from it all, and felt rather upset. I didn't think that I deserved to get bitten, and I couldn't believe what had just happened. It wasn't as if I had even stroked the dog. I think the dog must have been very hot and bad tempered, and decided to take it out on me. My mum was really worried because the dog had bitten through the skin, so she took me to the ambulance to get it checked out to see if I needed to have a tetanus jab. Luckily I was fine and for the rest of that day I stopped by my mum's side as I was a little shaken from it and felt a little sorry for myself. The rest of our time at the farm was really good. I even got to play with their Chinchilla and I also had a ride on one of their ponies.

A FRIGHTENED LITTLE GIRL

Only a few weeks later, things began to change and I noticed that my mum and Adam were constantly shouting at each other. I also noticed that he was spending a lot of time away at the weekends, after our family vacation and not a lot of time at home. Adam would go to the pub everyday and he would come back smelling of beer, which I hated.

Things started to change in our household very quickly and I could sense that mum and Adam were not getting along at all. By this time we had all grown really close to our step dad, who was usually very affectionate towards all of us, but sometimes that wasn't always the case.

This is the age where I was really beginning to remember a lot more and to notice a lot more. As I remember it, times weren't particularly nice in our household. Adam began to drink more heavily, and it was pretty frightening at times.

I had to be so responsible, which really wasn't very fair on me at such a young age. I believe now, that everything that happened at that stage, definitely made a huge impact on me. Sometimes I felt desperately upset and didn't really know how to deal with it all. I would cry and get upset when I was on my own, but didn't want anyone else to see me like that. I was scared to open up and I didn't want to create more problems.

I remember once, that Adam got so mad that he attempted to push my mum in rage, but I got in the way because I was trying to protect her. He knocked my head against the wall, and I had a lump on my head for days.

There was another incident when I was about eight years old. I can't fully remember what caused the argument, but I think Adam had driven across the garden in his Land Rover, which he had a habit of doing when he was in a drunken state of mind. Adam and my mum were arguing so angrily that I thought the best thing to do was call the police. I remember feeling petrified as I sneaked out of the house, and ran as fast as my little legs would carry me to the phone box. I felt as though my heart was in my mouth as I ran back down the hill and stood at the corner of the street until the police turned up.

When the police arrived, I ran up to tell them that my mum and Adam were inside the house and I was too scared to go back inside to see what had happened. So they put me into the back of the police car, and some time later they brought Adam out with handcuffs on. He saw me in the car and because he knew that I had called the police, he made a gun shape with his hand and then made a noise like he was shooting me. He also threatened to blow my brains out for doing what I'd done. I really can't believe that somebody could be so evil to such a young child. I was doing what I thought was the right thing and all I got was abuse thrown at me.

I was very worried because he actually owned guns, which were kept in my bedroom. It had been my mum's room before she moved into the next room with Adam, so that's why they were kept there. I had visions of him killing me, which was a real scary thought for an eight year old.

If you are in a violent relationship or a violent household, where this kind of thing takes place, then speak out. Don't let it carry on, because everyone suffers and nobody deserves such mental and physical abuse.

Physical violence and mental abuse happens everyday and there are thousands who feel they can't get out of the situation, but take my advice, be brave for yourself and for your children. There is help out there.

In my own case, there were times when things did get a bit tense and out of hand, but I learnt how to deal with it. Or perhaps I just put things to the back of my mind.

My mum was a great mum, and I wouldn't want her to feel guilty for what happened in the past, because I know she was in a difficult position and didn't know what to do. I now know she feels guilty about not doing more to get me away from that situation. We all make mistakes in our lives and that's what makes us human. I feel that domestic violence is a very serious issue, and it happens in a lot of families. Invariably the children are the ones that really suffer, as they can't speak out about it, or comprehend why adults behave in this way. It often has a huge long-term impact on their lives. I personally feel that these events affected me in a big way, even if I wasn't aware of it at the time. It usually shows later on in life, and in my case I think it may have contributed to leading me to the lifestyle I have today.

Up to that point, violence was not something that I had ever had to deal with. Nowadays, whenever I see violence or people in drunken states, it reminds me sometimes of how I grew up. I do get quite angry sometimes at the smallest things and I have to compose myself, but I have never become violently drunk. I don't really like the taste of alcohol and I only drink in small doses if I go out. However I know that alcohol often plays a big part when people get violent. Things weren't always so upsetting at home though.

A BABY BOY AND HORSES

One day my mum took me aside and asked me how much I would like a little brother or sister. I told her that I'd love it because I knew it would be great having a little playmate. That was the day she told me that she was having a baby boy. I remember feeling so excited because I had never been able to play with my sisters properly, as they were a lot older than me. There was only a year difference between them both, so they had a lot more in common.

Nine months went by and along came my brother. He had blond hair and blue eyes. Adam's granddad was called Gregory, so they decided on the name Gregory for my little brother. My mum was such an amazing lady. I don't know how she managed with having so many things to do. Mum was such a hard worker too. I really did appreciate any time that my mum and I managed to share together.

I recall one day that we were discussing hobbies, and she asked if I would like to try ballet. So I went along to a local hall and tried to fit in with what the others were doing. I didn't enjoy the experience, so my mum decided that I should try horse riding. There was a local horse riding stables just up the road, so my mum booked me in to have some lessons. All week I was eagerly looking forwards to my riding lessons. My mum bought me some jodhpurs and a pair of boots, and my dad gave me some money for my birthday, which I used to buy a hat and a whip. I had nervous butterflies in my stomach for the whole day because I was desperately hoping I would be good at riding. My lesson was booked for the late afternoon at the Hargrove Riding Stables, which were only five minutes away from home. There was a hut in the middle of the large yard with lots of stables surrounding it. There were loads of horses and ponies in their stables. In particular I noticed a little grey pony, and I immediately thought that I would be riding that one. At the side of the house there was an office where we had to book in with a riding instructor. The lady at the desk introduced herself as Jacqueline, and she asked me how much riding I had done before. I replied that I had only ridden a few times, but I had not had lessons before. My mum paid the fee and the lady told her to come back in an hour.

Boris, the horse, was around 13 hands and had such a lovely face. Jacqueline showed me how to do my stirrups and showed me how to get on. I instantly felt safe and ready to learn. I walked past the stable into a riding school where I began my first lesson. That's where I found my first love and the first time I felt I was good at something.

After a few more lessons at the riding school I asked if I could help out on a weekend and the lady said that this would be fine with her. The stables almost became my second home, and because I helped out so much they gave me free lessons. As time went on I was able to exercise the ponies myself because it all just came very natural to me. I loved everything about the farm. It was my little escape place where I learnt so much from spending so much time there. I even took lessons myself and taught children and adults sometimes. When times were bad at home and I had no one to talk to about what was going on, I would tack-up and go for a ride on my own in the local woods. I remember going as fast as I could, crying and praying. This happened on quite a few occasions. I was just trying to get all the frustration and sadness out in the open and I found that riding always helped.

I know now that I should have spoken to someone about how I felt, because it began to cause problems with my schoolwork and my concentration. My advice to any youngsters would be to try to speak to somebody for advice. Never bottle things up like I did.

I remember on one occasion that my friend Deanna and I sat at the dinner table eating Sunday lunch and we were giggling about something, like children do, when Adam came in and sat with us. He was far too drunk to even say anything as he fell into the dinning room chair clumsily. We continued joking and laughing, which seemed to offend Adam and he retaliated by throwing his dinner across the table.

At times like this I would escape to the place that I loved the most: to the horses and fields and the environment where I found tranquillity. But it seemed that even here I couldn't always escape mental or physical abuse. Maybe part of the problem was that I was so trusting and quite shy at times. The main problem was two girls at the stables, who were a few years older than myself. At times they weren't particularly nice to me. In fact they actually made my life hell up there. Sometimes I would go home in tears. On reflection I think it was some kind of power trip because one of the girls rode horses for the lady who took over the stables, and she was a bit more experienced than myself.

My mum told me to just ignore them. She knew how much I loved the stables and she found it quite frustrating to see me so upset, but the last thing I wanted was for her to go up there and say anything. I just put up with it and tried not to let it upset me. This was a form of bullying: not physical but mental. I know this sort of thing goes on every single day to thousands of people young people and adults. Some people suffer in silence and others are able to speak out, but either way the feelings always stay with you, and it sometimes causes problems in later life.

My solution was to pretend to carry on as normal and enjoy what I loved, even though deep down it was upsetting me on a daily basis.

Despite all the mental torture these girls inflicted on me I had some really fun times at the riding school. I was even entered into horse riding shows where I managed to win some rosettes. When that happened it felt like a real achievement to me, as I'd never really won anything like that at school. These events have stuck with me over all these years, and although I forgive all the people who acted so despicably, I will never forget what happened.

THE CARNIVAL

On one of our visits to my Nan's, my mum told me that we were going to watch the carnival. We walked into town as it was a really hot summer day and I was really eager to see all the pretty floats and the people parading around the streets. It was exactly how I imagined, and much more. My mum took us right to the top of one of the car parks where we could see everything. I could hear all the different music and people cheering as all the different floats went by. Amongst all sorts of floats there was one full of girls dressed up as princesses and a queen who sat at the front. They looked really pretty and I told my mum that I wanted to be like those girls in their pretty dresses. That particular image made an indelible impression on my young mind and focused my attention on something that I felt I could achieve.

My mum found out that I could be entered into a competition for the carnival, so that was exactly what I did. A few weeks later the competition would take place in the local hall. When I arrived there were a lot of girls around my age and also older ones who had entered the competition. There were also four judges sitting in a row. I felt apprehensive and nervous, but excited as well. We all took it in turns on a little stage where we were asked why we felt we would be good for our town carnival. Anyway a couple of hours went by and then the judges asked for everyone's attention because the winners were about to be announced. I couldn't believe it when I was the second name to be called. I felt overwhelmed, when I was handed a necklace, along with the other girls, it was lovely. I was going to be the next carnival princess and I couldn't wait. I hadn't been entered into such a big competition before, and I felt such a sense of achievement.

The lady, who was organising our team and the float, was really nice. She told us all that we needed to meet up the following weekend so the seamstress could take our measurements. We all met at a little cottage in the next village, which was about five minutes away from my house. I knocked on the door with a big black doorknocker and eventually a small elderly lady came to the door. She led us to a very small room where she asked for our names. When she heard mine she told me that she knew my mum.

She began taking all our measurements and told us that the dresses were going to be made in a shiny material. There were three princesses, so we would be in pink with little rose flowers at the tops of our shoulders. The queen would be wearing white and she would wear a large crown, whereas we would be wearing smaller tiaras. I was so excited and couldn't wait to see what was to follow a few weeks later when we went back for our dress fitting. At the final fitting she invited us into a room where we could try on our pink dresses. The first dress she picked up was mine. It was just what I imagined and I couldn't wait to get to wear it on the day of the carnival.

The big day came and we all met at Helen's house. Helen was organising our float and she was also pulling us along with her car. She was a very plain-looking lady, with short bobbed hair that was a very bright red in colour. She had a very exciting, bubbly personality that I liked. She told us that she would do all our hairstyles. I had kept my plaits in all night so that it was lovely and curly even though I had a natural wave to my hair anyway. She didn't really have much to do to my hair. She had only recently moved into a house that was nearly opposite our old house, so it reminded me so much of living in our old family home. The float was decorated with flowers and pretty writing along the side of the float. Helen reminded us we all needed to smile and to wave as though we were real royals.

Smiling is exactly what I did, even though I began to get jaw ache. People threw money onto the floats, and sometimes it hit me, but I just carried on smiling and enjoyed every minute. We had lots of pictures taken, and at the end of the day we would be judged against the other carnival queens from other towns. On this occasion myself and the other princesses won best carnival princesses of the day, so we were awarded a trophy. The next week our pictures were in our local newspaper, and somehow a modelling agency had seen my pictures and sent my mum some information on child modelling for catalogues. That was something I would have loved to do, but unfortunately it would have cost quite a bit of money to get a portfolio so we had to leave it.

I did the carnival for three years and loved ever minute of it. I also carried on with my horse riding as much as I could, even though I had to go to school. I would of much preferred to just ride everyday and not have to go to school. I longed to have my own horse, but unfortunately my mum couldn't afford one. Mum already had so much to pay for with the mortgage, living expenses for five people and all the other household bills that there was no possibility of paying for a horse as well. Even though mum had so much to pay for, and worked every hour God sent, she still managed to keep the family in a decent position. We always had food in the cupboards, new clothes, presents for Christmas and birthdays and a holiday every year abroad. My mum would often take us at weekends to the seaside or to a swimming pool or a country park for a picnic. Despite the fact that my mum was lone parent, she worked very hard to give us what every other normal family would have.

A BROKEN WRIST.

One year, my mum, my older sister, my little brother and myself planned a family holiday to go to Greece. My eldest sister decided not to come with the family, because she was old enough to stop at home by herself. By this time my mum and Adam had split up, and I was glad that they had. He had moved back to his mother's house, so our house returned to its former relaxed and calm state.

Two weeks before the family and I were due to leave, I had a show jumping event at the stables, and I was going to ride my favourite pony, which I had become really attached to. Julie, who I worked for up the stables, often brought and sold horses. Some of these horses even came from Holland, Belgium, and Spain. A couple of her own horses were good enough to be ridden at big international events. I remember when

Tammy, my pony, first arrived at the stables. Julie asked me to get on her to she what she was like. I was looking forwards to being the first person to try her out. I found some riding tack that would fit her and took it through to her stable, and then I walked her out to where there was a tree stump and pulled my stirrups down ready to get on her. The second I sat on Tammy I fell in love with her. Tammy was a grey Connor Mara: a very pretty looking pony with a very pretty face. I rode her around the arena and began to warm her up. She was a very elegant mare, and she stretched her legs out in an extended trot as I took her over the first jump that Julie had set up in the arena. Tammy looked really alert and with all the confidence in the world, over we went. Her previous owner had previously taken her foxhunting and cross-country, so Tammy could jump, but not exactly neat enough. Anyway I thought she would be fine around a small show jumping event. Julie said that I could ride her in the next show she was organising, and I agreed straight away, because I thought it would be great experience, even though it would be my first time riding in a show with a big audience.

On the day of the show, I made sure that Tammy looked as pretty as possible. She wasn't the best show jumping pony because she kind of leaped over the jumps. This was probably because she had done cross-country previously. We tried to do a bit of work on her before hand, but it's difficult to correct established habits, particularly as the animal gets older. There's a lot of truth in the old saying, "You can't teach an old dog new tricks." I was really nervous, because it was the first and biggest show I'd ever done. My mum said she would come along to watch and support me. I distinctly remember thinking that I looked the business in my cream Jodhpurs, polished black riding boots, and a posh grey riding jacket. I had to work out and remember what order the jumps were, and I hoped that Tammy wouldn't be a pain and become over excited. Anyway I climbed on her with some help from one of the other girls and walked her down the track towards the show arena, talking to her constantly. She heard the noise and started to prance a little knowing what was ahead. I just had to keep her as calm as possible so I took her into the warming up arena and cantered her around, and popped her over a few little jumps.

Ten minutes went by and then my name and Tammy's were called. Just at that point my mum arrived and wished me luck. I began to trot around the outside of the jumps and had my head focused on the first jump. I turned and held Tammy together, even though she was so excited by this time and started to pull a little. The first jump went well, and I thought to myself, great, come on we could do this. The second jump we approached also went well and I turned her to the next jump, which was a double. It was suppose to be a one-jump bounce and over the next, but it didn't work out like that. Tammy jumped the first and then unexpectedly paused sharply. I went over her head like super woman, and I heard the crowd gasp.

I was in shock, so I didn't really think about injuries. I just wanted to finish so much. I remember feeling rather silly, as this was the first time I had fallen off Tammy, and it was my bad luck to do it in front of an audience. I climbed back on and finished the round, but I had to turn her with only one hand. I was so determined to finish that I didn't realise that I had broken my wrist. I fought through the pain and was so relieved when I jumped the last fence.

It wasn't long after my accident at the show that I went on my family holiday to Greece, so I had to go with a big plaster cast on my wrist. It was really upsetting because I loved swimming and my plaster cast wasn't due to come off until the day after we returned from our holiday.

The holiday turned out to be great, even though I was a little disappointed at not being able to swim fully. In fact, I spent the week in a dingy floating about on the swimming pool instead. I was quite patient and uncomplaining over the time we were away, but I still hated the thought of my arm being white. I mentioned to my mum about removing the cast a little early. My mum said as it was suppose to come off in a couple of days anyway, and she couldn't see a problem with removing it as long as I felt that my wrist was better, and as long as we got it double checked when we got home. So we decided to chop the cast off, just so I could get some sun to it and also get one day in the swimming pool. I was slightly reluctant about it, but one of the guys that was also on his holidays helped out, and sawed it off with a knife. On reflection it was a bit stupid I know, but it felt so good at the same time. It had been itching like crazy as well.

MY FIRST BOYFRIEND

My eldest sister, Lucy, and I are a day apart with our birthdays. On my tenth birthday (Lucy's sixteenth) my dad organised a little birthday party for us both at the local pub. We had a birthday cake, with our names on, and a buffet, and when we arrived everyone sang to us. It was a really lovely and something that that I will always remember.

It wasn't long afterwards that Lucy fell pregnant. She was really quite upset about this, because she wanted to become a nurse and she felt that she would never be able to achieve her ambition if she had a baby. However, she decided to keep the baby, and to carry on to finish her exams at school. As it turned out, she did extremely well in her exams.

Her plan was to carry on with her education, and then when she had the baby, she would get my Nan to look after the baby while she was studying at college. This was her plan, and she stuck to it by the letter. She was determined not to let being a mother stop her from achieving what she wanted out of life. My Nan was really good to help Lucy through these difficult times. I admire anyone who continues with their education after having a child, and making a life for themselves.

In the end Lucy split from her partner, which was the best thing she could of done, because he was a bit of a 'head banger' and drank too much. He was constantly getting into fights with his brother and other people on a night out. On balance, Lucy was best out of it.

By the age of twelve I had already been in a middle school for three years. Most of the kids at my old primary school had gone on to the local school in our village. My mum gave me the option of going to a different school because I wasn't getting on well at my present school. I agreed, even though my present school was actually much nicer and the students were nicer too. The core problem was that I didn't enjoy going to school, and I didn't put enough effort into my work, which I really regret to this day.

Unfortunately, we can't turn back the clocks. We have to make the best of any position we find ourselves in. What ever goes wrong in life, as long as we focus our minds and keep trying, we will achieve what we want in the end.

I was entering my teens; the age where you want to explore and find out about as much as possible about the world and all that it offers. You could say that I did too much exploring and not enough thinking and working. I was too naive at the time to appreciate the dangers; a definite weak spot. Other than that, I was quite a fighter from an early age and I found from experience that I had to be prepared to defend my corner all through my growing up years. This has contributed to making me the adult I am today.

I was always a bit of a follower rather than a leader. I had a constant inner need to keep in with everybody, probably because I had so much trouble with trying to make and keep the right friends. I always blame this need as the cause of my starting smoking from the age of fourteen. My sisters thought it would be funny to let me have a puff a cigarette at eleven years old, but I don't think this was responsible for me taking up the habit so early. I remember they had a load of their friends around the house, and I think they thought it would be funny to offer me a smoke. I certainly didn't see the funny side because it nearly choked me! I forgive them now and I love them to bits, so it isn't something that bothers me.

When I started going out at the weekend, most of the groups of people I went around with were aged in their teens to their early twenties. Many within these groups were taking some form of drug. I am not sure if this was typical on a national scale, but it was certainly typical in my limited experience and from what I have seen in many youngsters in today's society. I didn't really understand anything to do with drugs at this age. My knowledge of drugs was less than negligible. I had heard some of the different names for them, and that the bad ones were; heroin, which you injected, and ecstasy, that could kill you. To be honest I hadn't paid attention or taken any notice at school during the little educational classes about drugs. I was just interested in dressing up and enjoying myself. I was blissfully unaware that I had an awful lot to learn – the hard way. In my ignorance I had to rely on what my friends said about taking drugs.

I had been asked on several occasions if I wanted a few 'blasts on a skunk joint' or a 'rocky joint', which was the local slang for cannabis, but at that time I wasn't really that bothered about trying it. Gradually I started going out more frequently, and at the same time I began to loose interest in my horses. I was only interested in getting dressed up and going out with all the young people I mixed with. After a night out, I began to feel hung over and wouldn't wake up in time to get a lift to the stables.

Most of girls in the groups I mixed with were a few years older than me and I really looked up to them. Several were 'doing base' (amphetamines), which they claimed would keep them up all night, and also give them a high. They would mainly 'bomb it', a local expression meaning swallowing the drug in one go, rolled up in a Rizla (cigarette) paper. Surrounded by such common use, it was inevitable that I began to try some of this and some of that.

I didn't have lots of girly friends, because I found it hard to handle when they were so nasty and bitchy at times about everybody. I couldn't be bothered with people like that. The few girl friends that I did have, would arrange for girly nights and we often got dressed up and went to the local football club. I loved getting dressed up, like most girls do, and by this time I looked much older than your average everyday fourteen year old.

I often got attention from young men, but I would always end up going home on my own. In contrast, many of the other girls would end up going off with guys round the corner, or even going home with them.

I also went around with a girl called Debbie, who was three years older than me, and she lived down the road, on the same street. She also went around with the same girl who caused me all my troubles at the stables. They went to school together, which is why they were such good friends. I actually wished she would just like me, because I had never done anything wrong to her. Her friendship with Debbie really upset me because sometimes, when we were out, she would try her hardest to get Debbie away from me. Sometimes she would do worse, and make Debbie cancel at the last minute when I'd got my self ready to go along to the football club disco. I have never met anyone else quite so spiteful. I couldn't understand why she was so mean, what was wrong with me? Was I boring? Or was it because I wasn't as old as they were? All these questions would torture my mind. Sometimes I would just sit alone at home hoping that they would change their mind, or if I could see anyone else out of the window that I could tag along with, so that my night wouldn't be totally spoilt. It got so bad that I began to get a bit of a complex.

I wasn't always going out with older groups. Sometimes I invited some of my friends from school to the disco, so it was nice to have some girls with me that were of the same age.

One evening I went to the Football club disco and met someone who made my heart melt. He was a real charmer and knew my name when he offered me a drink. How did he know my name and I didn't know his? I waited for him to come back over with my drink. I stood there, nervous and curious, wondering what was going to happen next. He came back to me as quick as he could, in a very assured manner, and passed me my drink and then kissed me on the cheek in a cool but charming way. I went over to one of my friends to ask them if they knew whom he was. She took one look at him and told me to keep clear and stay away. She had heard that he was trouble. I ignored this advice and decided to find out for myself. I have always seen the good in people, and I wanted to see what he was really like. I liked the look of him; he came across slightly flirty but caring. I instantly fell for him because of that.

We went up the Football club again the following week and I was having a great time dancing when Mick came over to me and asked me to accompany him in the last dance. I was really nervous, but I couldn't wait to slow dance with him. The music slowed down and Mick put his hands around my waist and mine around his shoulders and we danced to every song until the end when the lights came on. He asked if I wanted walking home and I agreed. Mick offered me his coat to keep me warm, because I was only wearing a little red silk dress that I loved. We talked to each other all the way home and I noticed a different side to him. He kissed me on the cheek when we finally reached my door and I told him that I would see him again, so we exchanged phone numbers.

THE BROWN POWDER

Mick and I began to see a lot of one another. All I could think and talk about was Mick when I wasn't with him. I was totally infatuated with him. Whenever I had the chance we would meet and go everywhere with each other. Sometimes I even bunked off school, here and there, so that we could spend time together. I even introduced him to my mum.

She really liked him because he was so out spoken. When I took him round to my house, he and my mum would always have lots to say to one another, which was nice.

One day Mick and I went to the next village with each other on the bus, to have a look around and also we wanted to do something outrageous. I wasn't old enough to have Mick's name tattooed on me because I was only fourteen, and he wasn't old enough to do the same, because he was only seventeen. In the end we decided on a piercing. We both had our noses pierced, but just on opposite sides. It wasn't something I would have wanted if Mick wasn't having it done, but I had this feeling of real happiness, because we had both done something together. This was the start of all the trouble with my father.

My father knew about Mick, and had also heard bad things about him. The story was that he was a drop out at school and he was a bit of a low life.

Bunking off school was becoming a bit of a habit, and the school rang my home to ask why I hadn't been in. I found out later on, that my dad had been around after work at my mum's house. He obviously found out that I hadn't gone to school and that I hadn't come back yet for tea. My dad got Mick's address and raced round to Mick's house and knocked on the door in a temper. Luckily Mick's mum and step dad weren't there on this occasion. Mick wanted to get in my dad's good books so he opened the door, which I thought it wasn't the brightest idea.

My dad demanded angrily that I return home immediately.

This was one of the few occasions that Mick acted responsibly. Other than that he was beginning to become a different person and his attitude towards me changed, and I couldn't understand why. I now realise that my father was only looking out for his daughter, like most fathers would do. When my dad saw what I had in my nose he pulled it out and told me it looked horrible. Since then I never put my nose stud back in.

Mick and I went out one day with his friend Terry who was slightly older than him, for a drive. We drove along the country roads near to where I lived, past all the stables with horses. I sat in the back of the car staring out while Mick talked with Terry about different kinds of music he liked. Mick wanted to roll a joint of marijuana, so we parked up along one of the back roads. I could smell something unusual and unlike the normal smell of pot. I leaned forwards to stroke the back of Mick's neck, and he snapped at me and told me to watch out because I nearly knocked him. I saw a piece of tin foil in his hand and sat there for a moment wondering what he could be doing. At first I thought he must have been doing cocaine or something like it, but I didn't dare ask just in case I made myself look stupid or in case he had one of his temper tantrums. In fact he was having these temper fits more and more often.

Mick fell out with his mum. At least that is what he told me, so he was living at his friend's house. He had known this particular family for years and he used their spare room. He invited me up there one afternoon, so I walked to the other side of town to see him. He sat there, again smoking some brown powder on tin foil, which seemed to bubble and smelt to me like burning stale fish. He walked into the kitchen and walked back with some butter in his hands. I just sat there, confused, and watching every move that Mick made, trying to understand what he was doing. He smudged a tiny bit of butter onto the foil and told me that it would run better and for longer.

He stood there towering over me, because he was a lot taller than I was, and seemed to find the whole situation hilarious. He asked me if I wanted to try some. It was like he wanted me to join in with his game. Maybe he found it funny seeing how I reacted when he offered it to me.

The situation and the circumstances seemed so ordinary that I thought to myself that there couldn't be any harm in it. If he was alright, then surely I would be. I trusted him. I didn't have a clue what it was that I was taking, but I suppose it was curiosity, and the ignorant naivety of youth that prevented me from seeing any harm. Certainly my conscience didn't raise any objections. So I put the foil tube in my mouth and began to inhale the smoke. It looked like a black beetle, a sticky looking blob running up and down the foil whilst I inhaled the smoke slowly. He asked me if it had done anything, and because I was so blissfully unaware, I had no idea what this stuff was supposed to be doing to me. I mean, what was I suppose to think, I didn't even know what I was taking, and I really couldn't see what all the fuss was about. I had noticed a change in Mick, in his personality, his temper, and the way he was treating me, but I didn't associate this with taking heroin.

For instance, one evening we were round the flat where one of Mick's friends lived on his own. He was disabled, because when he was younger he played 'chicken' in the road and didn't get out of the road in time. He was extremely overweight because of his disability, and he walked with a slight limp. You could definitely see Tomey a mile off because of his distinctive walk, as he was paralysed down one side, but he was a real character. It was a shame that Tomey had been so stupid, because he had to live with the consequences for the rest of his life. Tomey was a brilliant poet and could think of poems just like that. He would make up silly little poems about me, which always had me in fits of laughter. He was actually a really intelligent guy, but he was also a compulsive gambler. On this particular occasion

Mick was sitting there, chatting away, and putting some of that brown powder on to a piece of tin foil. I accidentally knocked against him and Mick nearly spilt some of it. He screamed at me and made a fist as if he wanted to hit me. I was so alarmed by his reaction that all I could do was keep apologising repeatedly. Within a couple of minutes Mick was all over me saying that he loved me and pulled me towards him in a firm cuddle. He was so up and down with his temper, it was like a complete personality change, and I didn't like it.

I was with Mick another time, and because he was so hyperactive at times, he would rush into things, which on this occasion caused an accident. We were messing around play fighting on the bed when Mick accidentally elbowed me in the nose causing it to bleed all over the place. I was beginning to not like his carelessness and I was beginning to see his true colours.

One time when Mick was visiting one of his friends, he had invited me along. There were also two brothers present. I had known the younger one for quite sometime, but I really didn't know much about the older one. One of my girly friends had been going out with the older brother, Pete. When I arrived at their house they were all sitting in the bedroom, and there was tin foil everywhere; on the floor, and on top of the cupboards. There black marks all over the place too. It wasn't a pretty sight to see. I had never been in such a dirty, untidy house like this before. They just sat there like zombies. Pete was actually dribbling all over himself and was not making sense at all. I was quite alarmed by all of this, as I hadn't seen anyone in this kind of state before. It actually frightened me, because he was acting so strange. I couldn't understand how my friend Lynda could even go out with a guy like this. He was about ten years older than she was and about thirteen years older than me. I sat there really quite dumb struck by these surroundings, when Lynda came in and I remember feeling very relieved, because at least I had somebody on the same wavelength as myself. Lynda was quite surprised to see me. She came across as a tomboy, but she actually wasn't. She came from a nice family home and lived in quite a big house with her mum and dad.

Pete called Lynda over to him and they started kissing, which I thought was pretty disgusting considering he had just been dribbling everywhere five minutes before and also coughing his saliva into cups that he had laying around the room. He passed her the foil tube and she begun to smoke this powder that was already all burnt down on the foil. It reminded me of a shiny beetle that kept on moving up and down the tin foil, which was moved by the heat of a cigarette lighter underneath. It was time for me to get home and Mick asked if I needed walking home. It wasn't far from where I lived, so I told him not to worry. He seemed pleased and had that empty vacant look about him (known locally as being out of it). I just wanted to get away from these people, who made me feel uneasy. Luckily Lynda was going home too so she said she would walk me half way.

On the way home I asked Lynda what they had been smoking back at the house, and to my surprise, she told me that it was heroin. I couldn't believe it, because I thought that you could only inject heroin. I tried to advise Lynda not to touch that stuff again, but I felt a bit of a hypocrite because I had tried it myself. She then told me that she wouldn't be going with Pete for long, and that she wouldn't be doing heroin again because she didn't think it was good for her.

Lynda's revelation didn't really sink in, probably because I just couldn't see or understand what real harm that heroin could do. It was a mystery to me, what all the fuss was about, and why people appeared so infatuated with doing heroin.

Things between Mick and I were beginning to get bad. To be honest, he was really getting me down. I thought about breaking up with him, and remembered how everybody had warned me about going with him. He did some real terrible things to me because he was using too much heroin. He didn't love me, he loved heroin, and it made him quite nasty.

One day, I remember when Mick didn't have any heroin, but he did have some methadone, which he had bought from someone. At that time I hadn't been taking heroin for very long, but it was beginning to become more of a routine, rather than a habit. He got one of his needles out and told me that if I didn't inject the methadone, then I would have to go without.

I didn't feel that I really needed to use anything at this point. I didn't realise at the time how dangerous this was. Methadone is supposed to be taken orally and never injected. How evil was Mick becoming? I was so innocent, how on earth was I supposed to know what this was going to do to me. Looking back, I don't even think that Mick knew the dangers either. Luckily, as I sat with my eyes closed crying with fear, Mick told me that the needle had blocked so he couldn't inject me. How irresponsible; he could have killed me.

AN UN EXPECTED OVERDOSE

It was a Friday night and I was getting ready with one of my new friends that Mick had introduced me to. Her name was Jess and she went out with a guy called Nick. They argued on every occasion that I turned up at their house. I never could work out what it was all about at the time, but I gathered later that it was always about the money that they were spending on drugs. Jess and I were getting all dressed up in our knee-high boots and little skirts and tops. Jess turned the stereo up as loud as she could and started dancing about, and began trying to teach me how to do a dance she had taught herself. She was dancing to 'happy hardcore', which is really fast music. The way she danced is very hard to explain, but it looked very professional.

Jess also smoked heroin and because we went out most Fridays together, she began to offer it to me. At first I would say no, but once I had taken it a few times with Mick, I felt obliged to accept her offer, because I thought she might think that I wasn't cool enough for her. I even asked her whether it would harm me or get me addicted. I was so frightened when taking it with Mick, that I wouldn't ask these questions. She told me not to be so stupid because she said that I would have to take loads to get a habit; like everyday for at least a month. At the time I had no idea what the implications of a habit were, and how dreadful it would feel.

So in the end I began taking it regularly with Jess. I had at least three lines up and down on the tin foil and began to get this felling, I felt warm around my whole body and it made me feel strangely full of energy but at the same time relaxed. I went to the toilet before I left the house and I remember looking in the mirror. I look slightly different; my eyes were glazed and my pupils were small, whereas usually at night they were quite large. I was pale and looked 'out of it', but at the same time I didn't really care. I just wanted to fit in and enjoy myself. Was that much too ask? On reflection after all these years, I suppose the answer has to be yes it was too much to ask, in view of the risk.

It was a Saturday and my mum was working at a nursing home in the next village. The elderly patients mostly had senile dementia, which made them quite difficult to look after. I had visited the home on several occasions and I always felt a little uncertain about how some of the patients reacted. There was one lady in particular who would often scream, shout and swear. My mum told me she was a very respectable lady in her time: a music teacher who would never swear or shout at other people. Her family mentioned to my mum that it was quite daunting and upsetting to see their mother in this way. There were a lot of patients in the same position. They were in no fit state of mind to be able to care for themselves. This was quite sad really. Some were incontinent, and it was very hard work taking care of these people.

I was fifteen now, and my mum asked me, if I would come in and help her, and she would pay me some money for doing so. By this time, my parents were starting to get stricter with me, and said they wanted me to stay away from Mick. So I rang him quickly to let him know what was going on. Mick answered and didn't really sound himself. He started to cry when I told him the situation, so I tried reassuring him by saying I would try and come round the following morning to speak to him. I was quite worried about him really. I had never heard him so 'out of it' and so depressed. I didn't know what to do, because I was at work in the nursing home at the time, so it left me worrying all day long.

It was a tough job really. We had to work in pairs, because one would have to lift while the other got the patient changed and ready for bed. There were not enough staff on this occasion, which was actually illegal, because we had to do twice as much work, and we were always supposed to have two people to do the lifting. By the end of the evening I felt extremely tired, both mentally and physically.

On the way home my mum told me that she was only acting in my best interests because I was getting behind at school, and I had not been myself since I had been going out with Mick. I really couldn't see that what she and my dad were doing was helping me. All I wanted to do was be with Mick, and because my mum and dad didn't want me to, it meant that I would have to do so without them knowing.

The next day and my mum went out somewhere. I woke up quite early, because all I could thing about was Mick. I couldn't call him because my mum had put a bar on the phone, so I decided to ride my mountain bike to use the phone box up the hill. At this time Mick had moved back home, so at least I knew where he would be.

The phone rang for quite a long time and I was just about to hang up when Mick answered, but I could barely hear him. I was frantic with worry because he sounded so strange. He was just making this peculiar noise down the phone and I couldn't understand what was wrong with him, so I climbed back on to my bike and rode as quickly as I could to the other end of town to see him. I was out of breath and began to cry. I was so worried, and I knew I wasn't suppose to be going near Mick, but I had to because I need to know what was wrong, and I believed that I was the only person who could help him.

My heart was beating so fast it felt as though it could have jumped out of my chest. I hadn't felt as bad as this since the time I ran to the phone box to report Adam. I ran up to the door of his house, and banged the door as loud as I could but there was no answer. I presumed his mum and step dad were at their weekend caravan. I knocked again and there was no answer, so I lifted the letterbox to see if I could see anything.

There was Mick, lying helplessly on the floor. I stood still for a second not knowing what to do. I had to think fast, so I ran over to the neighbour across the road to see if she knew what to do. Annie was a lovely lady, well built with rosy red cheeks. She answered the door and I began to speak at a million miles an hour, trying to explain what had happened. She told me to calm down, take a deep breath and to start again, so I tried explaining to her more clearly that Mick was lying on the floor and that there was something wrong with him. Annie calmly told me that she had a key and that she would call an ambulance.

I ran back to the house barely being able to get the key in the front door because I was shaking so much. I ran into the house and straight up to Mick. He lay there, looking grey and near to death.

A few minutes later the police turned up.

Then the ambulance arrived. I was so relieved. Within minutes Mick was on a stretcher and in the back of the ambulance. The medics began to ask me questions, and I didn't have any answers. I was so scared because I had never been in this position before and I didn't know what to do. They put a heart machine on and I could hear it making a beeping noise, and then they put the sirens on because they needed to get him to hospital as fast as possible. I asked the lady who was in the back of the ambulance what was wrong with Mick, and she replied that were not sure yet, but I need not worry.

I felt like I was going to pass out with all the worry and shock. I just felt so guilty because maybe this would not have happened if I had been there. In my innocence, I thought that this was entirely my fault.

They rushed Mick into the emergency room when we arrived at the hospital. They began to put machines on Mick again and they put a big needle in to his arm. The heart machine began to make that noise again, and the nurses ran around Mick trying to revive him. I felt so helpless, sad and numb. I didn't know what to do. I loved him so much and I just wanted things like they were when we first met. I couldn't work out why all this was happening. I was so relieved when they eventually got him stabilised.

A nurse took me to one side and told me what the problem was. Mick had taken an overdose and she wanted to know if he had ever tried taking his life before. I sat there feeling completely empty. Why would he want to kill himself? I just couldn't understand it. I was called into another room where Mick lay there awake. I ran over to try to cuddle and comfort him. I asked him how he felt, and he began to cry. He sat up, but he didn't look himself at all. His neck was bent over, like when someone has had a stroke. I dare not say anything just in case he took it the wrong way, and I didn't want to upset him.

Despite the fact that Mick had almost killed himself, it didn't stop him asking me to fill a needle with water. He took it out from his pocket and passed it to me. At this point I didn't really understand why he wanted a needle full of water. I assumed he knew what he was doing, so I filled it as best as I could and passed it back to him. I was puzzled by what he was doing and he told me he had a needle fixation. In effect, in his mind he was injecting heroin, but in practice it was only water.

He asked me to call his friend to get us a lift home, and it didn't take long for his friend to come and collect us. I was still worrying about how much trouble I was going to be in once I got home. I sat in the car not saying much, because I was still in shock about what I had been through. It had been such a stressful day. When we got back, Mick decided to go off with his mate, Waz. I needed to get home as quickly as possible, because I knew I was in real trouble and I didn't know what I was going to tell my mum. I just hoped she hadn't called my dad. I was still very much a child and I was thinking just like a child. I just hoped that they would understand why I had done what I had done.

I managed to sort things out with my parents, but they still told me to keep away from Mick because my schoolwork was more important. In truth I knew that my schoolwork and my motivation was virtually beyond recovery. I also knew that I was beginning to get a taste for the gear (heroin), which scared me because I still didn't really understand about drug addiction and how it ruins people's lives.

My mum had gone out for the day, so I thought I would invite Mick up to the house to break the news to him. I don't know how I found the strength to break up with him, but I knew it needed to be done. So when Mick arrived we went upstairs and he tried cuddling me and tried to kiss me as if there was nothing wrong. I remember feeling strangely calm as I told him that enough was enough. I wanted to stay friends but that was all. He just sat there for a second, looking straight through me, and then he began to cry. He told me that he needed and loved me, and wanted to spend the rest of his life with me. I was adamant that it had to stop. He then jumped up off of the bed where we were sitting and ran to the bathroom and locked him self inside.

He was hysterical, and shouted that if he couldn't have me, then he wanted to die. I was so stressed out with worry that it didn't dawn on me at the time, that this was selfish, blatant emotional blackmail. I tried pushing the door but he had locked it. In desperation, I put my full weight on the bottom door panel and my foot went through. I found Mick bent over the sink with blood over everything. It was just gushing from his wrists. I couldn't believe he had put me in this position. I had to apologise and say that I would stay with him. I just knew what he was capable of and it scared me. I felt alone in this situation, and felt as though my life was going from bad to worse.

It was about three weeks later and I was at a local 'doss house' where I thought I would find Mick, but this time I couldn't find him anywhere. No one knew where he was, and I just sat there waiting to see if he would eventually turn up. About two hours passed by and I knew that I would have to get home or my mum would wonder where I was. I sat chatting to three others that often visited this doss house, when one of Mick's friends came rushing in saying Mick and his brother Jamie had been arrested.

Mick's friend told us that Mick had been arrested for robbing a local bookmaker. I looked at him in disbelief, I thought he was having a joke, but he really wasn't. The most stupid part was that the bookmaker recognised Mick. I mean, how on earth wouldn't he recognise Mick, because he was so tall with a very distinctive voice, and he was a frequent visitor to the betting shop all the time.

In the end Mick and his accomplice were both found by police and remanded in custody. I couldn't believe it. I felt upset but relieved at the same time. I sat trying to get my head around all of this for about half an hour. I had really put up with more than enough and this was the last straw. I was far to young for all of this. All Mick had done was cause problem after problem. I decided to walk home where I found my mum sitting with a glass of wine in her hand, fast asleep with her head leaning over to one side. This was something I had put up with for years to come. My mum had put up with a lot of stress herself, but the state she was in didn't help matters when I needed to talk to her. In her defence, I think part of the problem may have been over work, because she needed more money for our holiday, and she was very lonely. Just after this dreadful nightmare, my mum booked the whole family a holiday in Turkey.

MY LAST FAMILY HOLIDAY

A few days later we were off to Turkey. Looking back, I think it was very fortuitous, because it allowed me to get away from the whole situation. I was really excited about getting away in the sun with the whole family. This would turn out to be the last holiday we had all together. As I packed, I remember thinking about recent events. I still felt I loved Mick, but I was a very mixed up youngster. I wasn't completely sure what I wanted. I had Mick's prison address, so I packed some writing paper so that I could write while I was away.

We arrived at the apartments that we were staying at and by this time it was the afternoon, but still very humid. We hadn't done anything like this since we were kids, and I really wanted to get to know my sisters better, now we were all growing up. The apartments we were staying at were lovely, with a huge swimming pool in the centre with all the apartments surrounding it. There was also a large bar, a room where they held discos and entertainment in the evening. We all had a lot to look forwards to, and it was so nice being with the people who I loved; my mum, my little brother, my Nan, my nephew and Karla.

It was so hot while we were there. I sat sun bathing and did quite a bit of swimming. This was the first time I began to notice the first signs of withdrawal symptoms while I was in Turkey. Until then I hadn't thought about it properly, because I was still very naive about the whole drug-taking scene at this point. My mum and I were talking to another couple on holiday, when I heard my mum tell them that our nice quiet village had recently had a problem with drugs, particularly heroin. At this point I kind of looked away and gulped because I had never heard her talk about such things before. I don't know why she brought up the subject but I didn't want to be a part of it. Later that day my nose started to run and I felt uneasy. It wasn't severe withdrawal, but it was the start and I sat thinking, maybe I've just got a cold coming or I'm run down after all the hassle with

Mick. It finally hit me, that maybe I was suffering from taking as much heroin as I had been. The following day I came on my period. This is something that usually happens every time I stop taking the gear (heroin). I think it's because heroin induces constipation. Once you stop using gear, everything else starts working again. I was hot, bothered and fed up because I knew I wouldn't be able to swim now that I had a period.

A fine holiday this was turning out to be. I was being denied all the things I was looking forwards to. It all seemed so unfair and left me feeling depressed and miserable, while the rest of my family were really enjoying themselves. I was just sitting there with my eyes closed, trying not to think about how I was feeling and minding my own business, when this young guy came over and picked me up and threw me into the swimming pool. I went under because it was so unexpected, and I swallowed quite a lot of water. I was so angry, even though the young Turkish guy was only playing around, because I wasn't feeling very well. Later that evening I sat on the veranda writing to Mick telling him that I was still in shock about the whole robbery situation. I told him where I was and that I would try to visit him soon. I would get a lift with his mum or a friend, because he was in a young offenders prison, about ninety minutes away. I told him that I was missing him, but when I sat and thought about the bad things he had got me into and encouraged me to do, I felt completely the opposite, and very angry.

My sister and mum came into my room and asked what I was up to, so I told them I was drawing, as I didn't want them to know that I was writing to Mick. I don't think they would have been very happy if I had told them the truth. My sister mentioned that there was a disco later and maybe an evening of fun would cheer me up. I hadn't had any real fun in ages. That evening was great. We all had a dance and I also found some admirers who wanted me to act in their production they were putting on a couple of nights later.

The night of the production came around and I sat waiting patiently to get called on stage. The mayor of the town came to watch, and after the applause and a standing ovation, the mayor spoke to my mum and I, to thank us for such a great evening. I told him that this wasn't something I actually did as a career, but he thought that I was so good that he would try to get me to work there. He also offered me the 'keys to the town', whatever that meant. My sister was a little 'off' with me while we were on that holiday. I will explain later why she had very good reasons to be like this.

I don't know where to start describing how much heartache and trouble that Mick caused my family and me. Mick had a reputation for being trouble with a capital 'T'. When he wanted to ruin things, he didn't mess about. You could say he was a real professional manipulator.

I'm actually sick in my stomach just writing this, because I've got to live with the guilt, after hurting my sister, Lucy, the way I did. I know she understands that I'm truly sorry now, but it still sticks in my head knowing that I was so stupid.

The trouble started while I was stopping at Lucy's for a week during the time I was with Mick. This was a few months before he went to prison and my trip away to Turkey. My father told me that I was no longer to see Mick and to stay out of his way. Lucy knew how I felt about him and told me that she didn't mind him coming round her place so I could get to see him. She knew that dad could be extremely strict and mean at times.

Well, to cut a long story short, Mick arrived around my sister's house late one afternoon. He was really please to see me, but I could see he had other things on his mind. Lucy wasn't actually there at the time. Mick sat down for a short time, and then stood up, and started pacing up and down the living room area, so I asked him what was wrong because I knew something was bothering him. He sat next to me and showed me a credit card that he had just picked up from Lucy's fireplace.

I remember looking at him in disbelief when he begged me to use it. He told me someone would kill him if he didn't pay his dealer off. Stupidly I believed his story, but I didn't know what to say because I knew it was wrong. He should not be asking me to do this. Then he started to pressurise and manipulate me even more, saying that my sister would get all the money back because the bank is insured. Was I stupid or what? Perhaps not stupid, but I was vulnerable and still very young. I believed every word that came out of his mouth. His eyes lit up as soon as he knew he had got me. He was like a leach. I remember doing exactly what he asked me to do, but I still had a horrible feeling about it. All I could do was question everything, but I just didn't have time to evaluate the situation or get out of it.

I walked down the road with Mick holding my hand tightly as he lead me on the path of wrong doing, until we came to the local shop around the corner from my sister's house. He told me to remember I was now Lucy Cesar, and to copy the signature on the card. This was in the days before chip and pin. I remember looking around the shop with my hands shaking and feeling perspiration under my top and around my neck. I had never felt so bad. I know it sounds wrong, but it kind of gave me an adrenalin rush too. I had never done anything like this before and I couldn't stop feeling so guilty and disgusted with myself. What was I thinking of? At the checkout I swiped the card through a machine and I signed a receipt. The girl behind the counter didn't even acknowledge me. It was as quick as that. I had done a terrible thing, just for that evil, selfish idiot.

I got arrested about a week later and was given a conditional discharge. My sister knew who was responsible, when she noticed her card had gone missing. Mick hadn't just tried to wreck my life, but he also nearly lost me my family. How destructive is that? Over the years I have tried more than anything to make things up to my sister. I know that I have not been the best sister because of my habit, but she knows and understands that sometimes people make stupid decisions.

It was about two days after retuning from Turkey that I received a letter from Mick, who said that he still missed me. Mick was under the age of 21 so he was sent to a young offenders institution. I'd heard terrible things about those particular prisons, so I was quite worried at the time. I heard that younger men would try and prove a point and get into fights. It seemed to me to be a lot worse than being in a men's prison. Even though I didn't like being parted from Mick I began to live my own life again: going out with friends and being able to be a normal teenager again. I also visited the stables because I really missed riding and doing what I loved.

A NEW FOOTBALLER BOYFRIEND

I was still dabbling with the gear (heroin) but not quite as much, because I didn't have much money at fifteen. I only had what I could earn and any pocket money my mum gave me. I still went out with Jess, but she didn't really share her heroin like she had before. She obviously needed it for herself and her boyfriend. I was still very young and vulnerable, and I still had a lot to learn. I had lost my motivation and interest in life and was beginning to drift into a world of drugs. Unfortunately, there was a lot more to come and I was completely oblivious of the approaching menace.

It was Friday night again, and I wanted to go out, even though half of me was reluctant, because of Mick being locked up. I felt quite guilty, because a lot of his letters indicated that he was paranoid about me leaving him. This wasn't something that didn't even cross my mind. I still felt that I loved him. In the end I decided to go out with my friends. Some of them were still not aware that I was taking an addictive drug. I had a great time and began to get some attention from a very attractive looking guy who was a year older than myself.

I had never looked at other guys because Mick was so obsessive. I couldn't stop looking at this gorgeous looking young man and he was doing very much the same to me. I found out that his name was Paul, and that he played football for the local team. He came across as very charming and he had a smile to die for.

One day he invited me around to his house, which was only about ten minutes from my house. The house was a gorgeous Manor house that looked like a giant castle. Well not quite as big as that, but a very big nevertheless. It was beautiful. I knocked on the door, which was opened by a very attractive, well dressed, middle age lady. She smiled sweetly and asked me if I wanted to speak to her son, Paul.

She called Paul to come down to greet me and then we went up to sit in his room where he showed me the pictures he had taken with Ryan Giggs. He also had a pair of football boots signed by Bobby Charlton. He told me that he had done trials for Sheffield United and he was very excited about this. I really enjoyed listening to Paul and what his ambitions were for his future.

He then asked me if I would like a little tour of his house. The house was wonderful. Down stairs there was a huge living room that had big wooden beams, and was decorated with great taste in lovely light colours. It had a big hallway that had a door leading to the part of the house occupied by his Gran and granddad, which had four bedrooms, a living room and kitchen. It was perfect for them both as they had help if they needed it and could live the rest of their lives close to their daughter.

The main house also had four large bedrooms. There was also a big conservatory on the back of the house, which lead to a lovely cottage kitchen. The upstairs had one level where Paul's room was, a spare room, and another room for his brother. This level also had a huge bathroom with a corner bath that Paul and his brother or guests could use. Opposite the bathroom were some wooden steps that curved round to another level where his parent's rooms were. They had a huge room where they could relax and watch television, and a stunning dressing room that any woman would die for. It had a shower and at the other end there was a bedroom fit for a king and queen. I was a really amazing and beautiful house.

He shared some little secrets with me, that I didn't know when I first met him. He told me that he smoked a bit of pot, but he was trying not to do it too often because it interfered with playing football and keeping fit. We spent a few hours together and then he walked me to the door to say goodbye. He kissed me and he said he would phone to see if I was going to the next football club disco. I walked away with butterflies in my stomach. I also felt very mixed up. I had seen another side of life and it was so different to life with Mick. I felt that I was making a huge mistake being with Mick, and I needed to think long and hard about how I was going to break the news to him, or was I going to wait?

The next day Mick gave me a call. We never had much to say to one another because he only had a little credit. He asked me if I was coming up to see him and if I had received his letter and prison visiting order. I told him that I had, so he said he would organise one of his friends to take me to see him. He also had something that I needed to bring with me to give him on the visit. I didn't really think about it at the time, but later, I started thinking what it could be?

At the weekend Terry collected me from my house and we drove to Leicester, which took us about an hour. Terry pulled over on the way and had some gear that he had already melted down onto the foil. He offered me a few lines and said to me that he had a small parcel of weed (cannabis) and some gear (heroin) that Mick wanted me to take into the prison for him. I couldn't believe that he was asking me to do such a stupid thing, but I also didn't want Mick to be angry with me. Terry told me that I should put it into my mouth and kiss him straight away when I got inside the prison. I really didn't know the implications of this, at sixteen years of age, but I felt scared because I knew that it was wrong and illegal. We pulled in to the car park of the prison, which looked horrible from the outside. It made me feel even more nervous and scared. I kept saying to Terry that I didn't like the idea and that I should leave it this time. In the end I ran back to the car to hide the drugs.

We walked in and presented our visiting orders and identification to the officer on the desk, and then a female warder patted me down and asked me open my mouth. Thank god I didn't go through with trying to get the drugs inside after all. I wasn't sure what kind of trouble I could have been in at that age, so I was very lucky. As we slowly walked through to the big hall I saw Mick sitting at the far side smiling like a Cheshire cat.

He jumped up shook Terry's hand and put his arms around me giving me a big kiss, and then looking at me with a big frown. I apologised, and told him that I couldn't do it until I had seen what the procedure was like coming in the first time. He looked so well, and I could see that he had been working out, because he asked the officer if he could take his jumper off. This left him with just a t-shirt, just so he could show off.

I was happy to see that Mick was looking more like himself again, and that he had his sense of humour back. He was holding onto a wooden box that he had made in his cell, and he passed it to me saying it had taken him ages to make it out of matchsticks. He had painted a big cannabis leaf on the front. It made me feel really good knowing that Mick had put the effort into making me something, although he did have all the time in the world.

I saw Mick another couple of times after that, but I never did try to smuggle drugs inside. On the third visit I noticed that he had a big cut above his lip, which he told me was the result of a punch-up with another young lad. It proved to me what others had told me about young guys in these young offender prisons. That wasn't the last time I went to visit Mick. I even went with his mum once, but by then he had moved to another prison that was a little closer.

BEING CONFUSED

It was another Friday night and I was going up the club to meet Paul and some of my friends. I got all dressed up and was really excited about seeing Paul. I knew that this was wrong, but at the same time I was angry about how Mick had treated me, and I just looking for the right moment to break up with him. I walked into the club and the first person I saw was Paul, he came over to me and gave me a kiss on the cheek and asked me how I was. Paul knew I was still with Mick and I was a bit worried that people would tell Mick about us as when he got out of prison. The last thing I wanted was for him to come and out and beat up Paul. I just hoped that didn't happen. I tried reassuring Paul and held his hand, but he was still a little worried.

Paul had been going around with a guy that did heroin and I was wondering whether he had taken some, because he looked as though he had. I didn't want to say anything and embarrass myself just in case I was wrong. The last thing I wanted to do was scare him off, but I could see it in his eyes. The eyes tell you many things, and they are a clear indication of heroin use. The pupils become very small (pinned) even in the dark. I thought I must have been mad to think that Paul would touch heroin because he had his football career ahead of him.

At the end of the evening Paul asked me if I wanted to go around to his house because his mum and dad were out, and he had some more drink in the cellar. I agreed, and we staggered back to his place, hand in hand, because we had both drunk little too much. I enjoyed Paul's company because we got on so well and he was quite a bit like me too. I really thought of him as a perfect boyfriend. I phoned my mum when I got to his house so that she wouldn't worry, and told her I was staying at a friend's house. Paul and I got very close that night, but all I could think about was Mick and how guilty I felt. In the end I told Paul that it wasn't the right time and we both just fell asleep in the spare room.

I went early the next day and when I got home I put on a song that was a favourite of mine. It's funny how certain songs remind you of people, places or a time in your life that was either sad or good. I began to cry and I felt so alone. My emotions were out of control and I felt that everything was going from bad to worse. I just didn't know what to do. I wanted heroin more and more, and school wasn't going well. I could tell that people at school were beginning to talk about me taking drugs. The only person at school who knew was my best friend Andrea, and on a couple of occasions she would have a couple of lines with me in the toilets. Most of all, Mick played on my mind and I couldn't cope with it. Why was this happening to me and what had I done to deserve all of this? I lay there trying to work things out, holding on to one of my old teddy bears like an upset child that just needs a cuddle and some reassurance that things would get better. I felt I couldn't confide in anyone because I wasn't sure how my friends would react. I convinced myself that things would work out, and I eventually fell into a deep sleep.

I dreamt about riding a beautiful white horse that took me away from everything that had been happening and dragging me down, to a place that was just beautiful, I felt an overwhelming sense of joy, as I lay there asleep. Just as it began to get better I woke up realising it was just a dream. Usually, I would dream about horrible situations that were happening in my life.

The time was getting closer to Mick's release and I was still seeing Paul. I was taking a lot more gear (heroin), even to the point where I took it to school with me to use in the girl's toilets. I really didn't know where I was going with things, and times were getting really dangerous. My future and my life were looking decidedly grim.

Paul and I spent more and more time with each other, and I was right when I suspected that he was dabbling with the gear. I saw him with some guys early one morning, rushing as quickly as they could, to get some gear. It just meant that we started taking it quite frequently together. Paul told me he needed some so that he could get himself to college, because he had started an electrical and plumbing course. He wanted to have a trade and a good career a head of him if football didn't work out. Paul would also be able to take on his dad's business one day, because eventually it would get passed down to Paul and his brother. I went around to Paul's house most evenings and we began 'using' (taking heroin) together more and more, because Paul could always get money. We would often get around fifty pounds worth and we sat and shared it. This gradually becomes a way of life; a routine that become a habit in its own right.

I'd been out one day and brought two bags of gear (£20 pounds), and rushed straight home so that I could begin to smoke them, I went into the cupboard to get some tin foil and then went back in to my bedroom to have a smoke. I was probably being a little careless at this time. Lucy had already moved in with her husband to be, and Karla my other sister was living with her friend in the next town, which just left my little brother, my mum and myself at home. Nobody was at home at this point, and then suddenly my mum flew into the bedroom with a very red face. She was angrier than I had seen her in a long while. I was taken off guard completely by her coming in like she did, and she began to shout at me hysterically. I felt so guilty that I was lost for words and just sat there. She was so mad, she pulled my top and push me, so I stood up and tried to calm her down. There was no stopping her as she grabbed my foil and screwed it up into a ball. That was when she told me how she knew what I was doing.

I was in shock, and she knew that I couldn't get out of it. Apparently, the lady who worked at our local petrol garage had informed her what I was doing. I thought this was a somewhat hypocritical situation because the lady's son was also a heroin user, but she didn't say a word to my mum about that. I was getting my heroin at the time from a guy who lived opposite the garage, so the lady was keeping watch on everyone who went to the house.

My mum was furious, and all I could do was apologise to her. I was crying and felt extremely guilty that I had upset her so much. At this time I wasn't accustomed to worming my way out of things, so that's why I admitted exactly what had been going on. When my mum left the room, I sat there thinking what a complete idiot I had been. How could I have been so careless?

My mum took the heroin on the foil, with her, and shouted up the stairs to me that she was going to call the police. At the time, my mum was completely clueless and uneducated about anything to do with drugs, so she had no idea how to deal with the situation. I was petrified and totally unaware of what was going to happen next, I had never been in trouble before with the police, so this really worried me. My mum called me downstairs shortly afterwards, and I could hear the policeman's radio making lots of noise as I approached the living room. My mum was talking slowly by this time, and explained what had happened. He just advised me to talk to my mum and get the problem sorted out with the drug advisory service to stop. He was actually one of the better policemen we had at the time. Heroin hadn't been in the town long, so the police were not familiar with users and how to deal with that particular situation. I felt sure he wasn't there to cause trouble, but to help and give some support. The foil didn't concern him one bit, he just left it sitting there and carried on talking to my mum. After about thirty minutes he left and my mum had a calm chat with me.

My mum had a long talk to me that evening and said that she would help me stop, but she needed to find out how things stood with me being only sixteen and whether I would get help from the NHS. I was so upset by everything that had happened that I went to my room and waited until my mum went to bed. I lay there feeling ill, as I hadn't been able to have any gear; I was confused and felt a desperately guilty. I wasn't ready to admit that I was an addict, but I did realised that I had got myself into something serious. Later I went back to the bin where my mum had thrown the screwed up tin foil to see if I could salvage any. I was nervous because I didn't want my mum to catch me out again. I am convinced that she would have killed me. I carefully rummaged through the rubbish and found the foil. There was a very small amount on the foil, so I carefully flattened it and then went into the living room to finish it, because I thought my mum would have heard the sound of the tin foil in my bedroom. Afterwards I found some deodorant to spray about so that the smell would be gone by the morning.

A couple of weeks went by after my mum caught me using. Mick was due out of prison. We hadn't really spoken to one another, after someone had told him that I was going out with Paul. Part of me wanted to see Mick, but I really didn't know what I wanted. I walked up to a house were I thought Mick might go as I had a feeling that he would come out of prison and start using straight away. I knocked the door and asked if anyone had seen him, but nobody had, so I then went his mums to see if he was there. His step dad told me that he had gone shopping for clothes with his mum. I felt disappointed, and returned home to find Mick was waiting outside my house. He still looked pleased to see me considering the circumstances and he gave me a big cuddle and said that he had missed me. That day we spent a few hours together and I told him what was going on and that I needed some time to get my act together.

We carried on seeing each other for another few weeks until I found out that Mick had seen another girl behind my back. Even though I knew that I had done the same to him, I still couldn't help feeling annoyed and betrayed. He told me he had done in out of spite, and he didn't actually have feelings for this girl at all. He had lied so often in the past that I decided to check out whether they were actually seeing one another or not. That evening I went to the local fair because I had been told that this was how Mick met her. When I got to the fair I walked around trying to find some familiar faces, and that's when I saw Mick standing there with this girl. I ran over shouting with anger. You could say that this was a case of 'the pot calling the kettle black', but I was so wound up and emotionally disturbed that I couldn't recognise 'fairness and reason' even if it poked me in the eyes. I wasn't normally a violent person, but I slapped Mick and pushed this girl. Mick grabbed hold of me really tightly and told me to calm down, but I just felt so angry. Mick clearly had no understanding of how much he had pressured me, and casually stood there with not a care in the world. I walked away, telling Mick it was over and I didn't ever want to see him again.

The next day Mick met me outside the school, and asked if I wanted to go and have some gear with him, because he wanted to talk. I decided to go with him just so that I could hear what rubbish and lies he had to tell me. I also knew he was a very good manipulator, because that's what he had done to me all the way through our relationship. I realised that there was only one thing that was important to Mick: heroin. I told him we ought to stay away from each other, and that's exactly what he did. I have to admit that this surprised me. I knew in my heart that it wouldn't be long before Mick would be fully back on the gear, and back to doing bad things, and I was right. Mick deteriorated really quickly, and it didn't take long for him to start looking like an addict again. He also went back to his old tricks; stealing off friends that were non-users, and also doing burglaries. I saw him on one occasion on crutches as he had given himself an abscess and he could barely walk, he was in a real mess. It didn't take him long before he was back inside prison after that.

I knew that I urgently needed to get well again, but I also knew it wasn't going to be easy. I couldn't afford to continue smoking heroin so I began to inject, even though I found it very unpleasant. Most people are a bit squeamish about having injections. Nobody likes them. Injecting yourself is infinitely worse. Desperate people do desperate things. Mum worked hard to educate herself about drugs, in particular heroin. She knew that when I hadn't got heroin I couldn't function or even cope with the withdrawal symptoms. I simply fell apart and became virtually mentally unstable in some respects. Basically I needed heroin from the first moment my eyes open until I fell asleep at night. Some mornings I would get myself in a real state because I wasn't the best at injecting myself. To be honest, I hadn't been doing it long enough. I had never been taught how to do it so I just copied other people. Mum would often walk into my room to find me crying my eyes out in frustration and desperation. I often had blood all the way down my t-shirt that I had been wearing in bed. It was very upsetting for her to see me, and I felt terrible because my mum had seen me in this way. My mum decided to help me out with a little money, until I was able to get myself off of it. I begged her when I first got up in he morning, because I would be rattling (feeling rotten) for some gear. This was the only thing in my mind. Nothing else mattered until I had my fix. I needed to make myself feel better and more like a normal person.

You might be thinking that this girl must be an idiot. She has just given the elbow to a real nasty piece of work: a guy who had turned her into an addict, and now she has taken up with another one. The only defence I can offer is that I was still very young and drugs had significantly impaired my ability to think rationally. Desperation causes you to do many stupid things in life, I was clinging onto people that were also making the same terrible mistakes that I was making.

BEING ON TV

In her quest to find help for me, my mum called some television program makers. The problem was that there wasn't any help for drug users under the age of sixteen on the NHS. My mum wanted to campaign to rectify this blatant omission in the National Health Service. This was becoming an increasingly important issue because more and more young people were becoming addicted to hard drugs. She planned for both of us to appear on one of the popular national TV programs to see if she could get some help for me and for others like me. At the time I didn't feel that going on TV would be a problem, but only later did I realised that it probably did me more harm than good. As a result of my mum's efforts we ended up going to a TV studio in London. They put us in a hotel the night before because we had to get up very early the next morning to get a taxi to the studio. The hotel was really nice and they also paid for us to have a meal. My mum woke me very early the next morning in time to get a cab to the studio. They sat us in the green room and said that there were plenty of things to eat if we wanted to help ourselves. The program was being made in one of the biggest television studios, which was quite intimidating and made me nervous, but at the same time it was quite exciting.

They asked if I would like my make-up touching up and I agreed, I'd never had my make-up done by a professional make-up artist. One of the program presenters who was having her make-up done, didn't even look at me and I felt that she was being quite rude. Instantly I thought that this was because she knew that I was, a smack head, a junkie, a heroin addict. These are some of the names that people call an addict and which I find very hurtful and judgmental. Why do people have to label us in this way? I'm only human like the next person. You might say that I was making assumptions and being paranoid about what people were thinking, but that is what heroin does to people. I like to read, and I often read autobiographies of famous people. I think that is what inspired me to write my own life story, even though I am not famous.

Eventually I was called through to the studio where I sat with my mum and the two presenters. They were very nice and they asked me questions about wanting to come off of heroin and what we thought about the absence of help for young drug users under the age of sixteen on the NHS. I also explained a little about my life before heroin, and I also explained about an implant treatment that I was available privately.

We only knew a little about the Naltrexone implants at this stage, but we had heard that it was 100 % successful in helping addicts to keep off heroin once they had done a detox. The treatment only works when the body is completely clear of opiates including; heroin, dihydrocodeine, Subutex, methadone or anything else that contains opiates. The flaw in the whole process is the detox (clearing out the opiates). This the most painful and difficult part: the part that deters most addicts from even trying to get clean. Naltrexone is fine for keeping people off heroin once they are clean.

Later on I found out a lot more information about Naltrexone. It can be taken orally or inserted into the groin area under local anaesthetic. The implants last six to seven weeks depending on the individual because it dissolves differently with each person. There are also six-month implants. The drug works by connecting itself to the nerve endings in the head and it acts as a blocker to stop heroin getting in. So this was another option and something my family thought about.

After I had been on the television show I was bombarded with news reporters and different TV shows, asking if I would talk further about my situation. I went on the news too, but the sudden notoriety was extremely stressful so I asked my mum to ask them to leave because I wasn't interested in doing any further interviews. It was so tiring, and I began to regret it, because those people that didn't previously know I was an addict now knew. I had to face them knowing that they were going to ask questions and judge me for being a drug user. To them I was just another 'druggie', but my close friends and family, all knew that it was an illness: a very serious illness.

Most people don't realise that drug addiction is an illness that is every bit as real and dangerous as say, anorexia. I suppose it isn't their fault because drug addicts don't get good press coverage, probably because it is widely considered a self-inflicted condition. Nevertheless, it is an illness with so many different mental and physical symptoms. Heroin is both mentally and physically addictive, and extremely difficult to conquer. I wouldn't wish it on anybody. Of course it is possible to stop using the drug, but the addiction never goes away and haunts you and your family for the rest of your life in some form or other.

About a week after I had been on the television news and after I appeared in the 'Women's Own' magazine, I was in a position to reflect on this experience. I didn't do any of it for money: it was a cry for help for me and for others like me. I was left feeling empty and quite upset that I had revealed myself to the world in order to help others. I would now have to suffer the consequences every time I walked down the main high street. People would turn and start talking about me being the local 'druggie' and people that spoke to me before would no longer speak to me. I found this very difficult to handle because I had always suffered from wanting people to like me. It seemed as though my TV appearance was a free ticket for people to judge me and criticise me before they knew all the facts.

The one good thing that came out of my TV appearance was that it might have contributed to a change in the NHS rules that allowed youngsters of any age to receive treatment for drug addiction.

I had to have a meeting with the local 'drug and alcohol abuse' services to get me on to my first ever detox programme. I also had a meeting with the head master at school to discuss what was best for my future. It was all quite awkward really because my head master thought that I was going to be a problem for the reputation of the school. He had come to the conclusion that I needed to leave as I had missed so much schoolwork anyway. This was another unforeseen repercussion from my moment of TV 'fame'.

What I thought he should have done was to give me time to get onto a detox programme until I was feeling stronger, and then let me come back to finish my education, or even try and give me some extra classes after school hours. Clearly the reputation of the school came before my personal welfare. His decision was stupid, counter productive and didn't help my situation at all. Previously my attendance at school was erratic but at least I did turn up some of the time, whereas expelling me meant I would now be at home all of the time. This gave me all the time in the world to do even more of what I was doing previously.

I had to wait quite a while as there was quite a long waiting list to see the doctor to discuss a prescription that would be suitable for me, and also to get a date to begin titrations to get me stable on medication.

During this time Paul and I were spending a lot of time together, and doing as much gear as we could get are hands on, or to be more precise, how much cash we could get our hands on. Paul had previously been for a football trial and had got down to the last sixteen, but after few months he began to loose interest. Paul didn't get chosen to play for Sheffield United, which undermined his determination. I think deep down it got to him more than he let on. He didn't seem to realise that you can't smoke and do drugs and expect to become a professional footballer at the same time. It was a real shame, because he could have been another Beckham. He was a very stylish lad, and extremely good at football, and he also had the support of his family to encouraged him, but he lost it all. Heroin is a great de-motivator.

We were always 'ducking and diving' (avoiding the police), another aspect of life on the gear. It was going to be a long time before I eventually stopped the gear because there was a huge waiting list to start a detox programme. I seriously doubted that I could last out that long because things were already too much for me to handle.

My family talked about me going to a religious detox centre, not because it was a religious one, but because they were the only ones available at the time that were free. Even so it made me feel as though I was being pushed into something I didn't want to do. I was still a very young and insecure girl who needed the people she loved and cared for around her. My family thought it was in my best interests, because they realised that doing a detox was one thing, whereas keeping me away from temptation afterwards was quite another. Perhaps I wasn't ready to face up to the stark realities of my situation; that money and circumstances essentially excluded my own preferences.

A week later my mum told me there was a place for me at a centre in Wiltshire where I would have to stay for 6 months. It was a huge mansion that had been converted into a detox centre for young people who needed help after being on drugs or alcohol. The thought of it made me feel empty, as though nobody wanted me around, and I definitely didn't want to go. The thought of having to leave home had a huge impact on me that day. I was already in a very fragile state and these thoughts more or less tipped me over the edge. I sat on the end of my bed in a daze, scared and on the verge of panic, when I looked over at my bottle of sleeping tablets on the bedside table. I suppose it was desperation, but in a mad moment, I picked up the bottle up and took some tablets and before I knew it I had taken them all. Immediately afterwards I couldn't believe what I had just done. I took around thirty tablets to be exact. I was scared rigid and just sat on my bed crying, not knowing what would happen next. I had this terrible feeling in my stomach and began to have a panic attack. I know this sounds bizarre but I was only a child rebelling. I didn't really want to die, I just wanted a way out and that was the only way I thought people would listen. It was a cry for help: a cry to say please don't make me go.

My dad came around to see if I was ready for my time away, and came upstairs to speak to me. I sat there with the bottle in my hands and all I kept on doing was apologising. He looked at me in sheer terror when he realised what I had done. My mum heard all the commotion because I was crying so loudly and knew straight away that something was going on and rushed to my room. My mum and dad stood there riddled with worry and guilt. They rushed me to hospital as quick as they could and by the time I got there I passed out and didn't wake up until many hours later. My dad sat next to me waiting for me to wake up and told me that I was going to be all right. Fortunately I had slept the tablets off and didn't need to have my stomach pumped. I can only blame myself for this really upsetting experience, but at least it gave me a chance to tell them exactly how I felt.

LIVING IN A SHED

People with shared interests and experiences tend to congregate together in groups, like immigrants, football supporters and cigarette smokers. This is true of drug users too, and because it is illegal it is no surprise that this group tends to attract some very unsavoury characters (wrong-uns).

A guy called Louigi offered Paul and me to stop at his flat. Obviously by his name, you can tell that he has some Italian in him, even though he has never been there and cannot speak any Italian. He was a short, scruffy looking guy who was always scratching his head. To be honest I don't think he had bathed in a long while. I made sure that I didn't get close enough to find out, because he smelt quite bad when he passed by. It was really quite embarrassing that we were reduced to stopping in such places. After all, we had both been brought up in clean and decent homes.

What was heroin turning us into? We were on the verge of becoming exactly like the stereotypical image of drug users.

This was probably the start of our bad times, as if our addictions weren't bad enough already. We kept Louigi's offer in mind for a few weeks after staying somewhere else. It was the summer of 1998, and I had been doing a little work at the nursing home again. Paul and I wanted to stay together at night, because it was extremely difficult to get across town to pick up our gear everyday. Paul had a crazy idea to sleep in the shed at the side of the Manor house, because we had nowhere else to stay at this point. The shed even had electricity, because Paul's dad and brother had an electrical business, and we put plenty of quilts in there to keep us warm.

We were hoping that no one would find out that we were going to stay in there, so we knew we had to be very careful. There were spiders crawling about that kept me up most of the time, but it was bearable and quite warm in the middle of summer. Paul told his mum, that he was stopping with friends so that he could get some extra money from her: another terrible lie to add to the others that we had to tell every day. He told her that we needed it for food and rent where we were staying.

Life in the garden shed was a surreal experience. We were stopping in the shed at night and then sneaking around the front of the house in the morning and knocking the door to have a shower and breakfast in this beautiful six bedroom Manor House.

We were also good friends with a guy who was selling heroin on his rounds as a milkman and would deliver it to the Manor was on his round. We would leave the cash in the milk holder for him early in the morning with a note to ask if he could leave some milk, fresh orange and bread, and leave our gear at the same time. It was very convenient and crazy to look back on. If Paul's mum wasn't in when we woke up, we would just have a wash from the outside tap to freshen up until we could shower ourselves later. We didn't do this for long because we took up the offer of Louigi's flat.

Louigi told us that we could use the roof of his flat because it was all converted and safe to do so. The actual flat itself was pretty horrid, but with a little hard work we made it liveable and clean. The tiny room had a skylight window that let in fresh air and plenty of light.

We were both on our way home one day walking through the main high street by the bank, where there were a lot of steps that lead to the flat, when we saw two people running towards us. Paul recognised them as the local police dressed in civilian clothes. We had seen them before and even chatted to them on a few occasions. Paul was carrying gear and didn't want to be arrested so he attempted to throw our gear away. It was so obvious that he was throwing it away that they stopped and searched us. They had seen us rushing down the street and because Paul had a carrier bag they decided to investigate. In fact they thought we had been shoplifting, which is why they followed us. At that time we didn't do shoplifting because Paul could get money quite easily from his parents. The police hunted around for the gear for about fifteen minutes. They were convinced it was in the bushes and they weren't giving up until they found it. Eventually one of them did find it, so they arrested Paul for possession.

In the early days I actually liked the police because they spoke to us like human beings and they were pretty fair. When they treat you like that, you co-operate, but it when they treat you unfairly then you lose respect for them. In those days they would ask how we were getting on, and if we were getting help and treatment. Nowadays, the police are just out to lock you up and make you feel like crap. Don't they realise we are basically just like them except but we have just got ourselves in a bad position which is very hard to get away from. I don't think they really care.

We didn't stay at the flat for much longer because there was trouble all the time around there. One day we all ended up getting arrested for stolen goods being in the flat. Basically, if stolen goods are found on the premises then everyone gets tarred with the same brush, so we had to spend a day in the cells, even though we had nothing to do with it.

It had come to the point where our families noticed that the pattern of our behaviour had changed. They were both extremely worried and questioned us numerous times. Both our families wanted to try and help us get things sorted out. Now that both our parents knew about our drug habit, they tried their hardest to help us tackle it. Once again we had a long wait before we went through the process of getting medication at our local drug and rehabilitation centre.

One day, Paul and I were invited to go to a Lotus car show. The idea was to keep us busy and to have a nice day out at the same time. Paul's dad was a lover of cars and he owned his own bright red Lotus sports car. We both climbed awkwardly into the back because it wasn't very spacious. The car even had bucket seats like a real racing car. It always felt very grand driving away from Paul's house because it even had an electric gate, which his dad opened with a control in his car. It was a beautiful hot summer day, and there were lots of sleek Lotus cars outside. We were able to sit in some of the cars and we also had something to eat while we were there.

We went to a lot of car shows with Paul's mum and dad. Cheryl, Paul's mother, also did a lot of charity work for Dr Barnardos. She often held very grand garden parties, complete with a buffet. We were told we could help ourselves to some food, and then we would sit up in Paul's bedroom out of the way. I often looked down enviously on all these very posh people in the garden. Most of the women had beautiful jewellery and were very well dressed. The men usually wore smart trousers and ties. Sometimes I overheard people saying that I was such a pretty girl and that Paul was a very lucky chap. Cheryl had also been a stage performer while she was growing up. There were lots of picture of her shows on the wall, which I found fascinating, and I often wished that I had done something similar. I admire people that do anything like that. It is so inspiring.

NEAR TO DEATH

One day, Paul and I went around to another doss house where people sat and smoked heroin. A guy called David lived there. We were both injected at this point, so we got out our spoon and injecting equipment. There weren't many people round there on this occasion: one of the guys I had not seen before, and there were two others that I knew from seeing them around our town. I was listening to this particular guy chatting away in his Cockney accent. He was quite a large, bald headed man, with a rough appearance. He made me feel slightly unsettled and intimidated.

David had just got onto the subject of his mum nearly throwing him out because he had basically stolen everything in the house. I'm not sure what he meant by everything, but that's how he described it, and he had apparently left the house nearly bare. Personally I found this difficult to believe because there was still furniture and other things in the living room. People on drugs have a tendency to exaggerate so you learn to allow for this. Even so I couldn't believe that he could have done this, because he was a really quite reserved young guy and it wasn't as if they had a great house full of expensive things. In fact it smelt of dogs and the carpets and furniture were old. He said how lucky he had been that his mum was so forgiving, after doing such a terrible thing to his own mother while she was away on her holiday.

The guy with the cockney accent introduced himself as Lee and he told us that he hadn't long been out of prison but I got the impression that he was 'a billy-bull-shitter' (someone who had a tendency to lie). I also noticed while he was introducing himself that he had a needle in his hand. Within a matter of seconds, he suddenly went from a sitting up position to a slouched position. He had only had about five pounds worth of heroin in his needle because I heard him arguing with David when they divided a ten-pound bag in half. About a minute later he was fully bent over with the needle sticking out of his hand, with blood dripping onto the carpet and he was turning purple. I instantly knew that this was serious and he was going to die if somebody didn't help him.

There was sheer panic in the room. Nobody was doing a thing to help Lee. This not surprising because calling an ambulance would be to invite trouble. Inevitably the police would turn up and nobody wanted to lose their gear and get arrested. As a result the person who was over-dosing would be left alone to die. Most of the people left the house, leaving Paul and me to deal with Lee. He was such a big heavy guy that it was impossible to move him, and by this point he was in a position where he could have easily suffocated. He was also making a loud noise as if there was something wrong with his breathing. We eventually managed to pull him off the chair and laid him flat on the floor so that we could try to push his head back to keep his airways clear. I didn't really know first aid at this stage so I did what I thought was common sense.

Meanwhile David called an ambulance, which arrived about five minutes later. Fortunately the police didn't turn up as well. I was so relieved to see some medical assistance because Lee was so close to death and there was nothing I could have done. It was really scary because I had never seen anything like this before. The paramedics asked what he had taken, so I told them. The paramedics couldn't find a vein in his body anywhere at first and they knew it was a crucial situation with no time to mess about. Eventually they found a vein in his neck and then they apparently used adrenaline to bring him round.

In an instant after injecting him, Lee made a big gasping noise and there he was, eyes wide open, really disoriented and confused by what was going on. The paramedics had to reassure him and calm him down because he began to get restless and kept trying to get up. There was a strange look to him for around ten minutes afterwards: like his eyes were popping out of his head. I had seen something like it in one of the patients in the nursing home who had senile dementia. The paramedics told him that he was close to death and that he needed to think a bit more before doing that again.

They left shortly afterwards, once they could see that Lee would recover. Lee was in shock afterwards, because he couldn't believe what had just happened to him. He had told us later that he hadn't been using heroin regularly everyday and this was probably why his tolerance was so low. Despite this dramatic and dangerous episode, it still didn't stop the mental and physical craving I have for heroin: it is so overpowering.

As you can clearly see, heroin addiction isn't just a simple case of taking the drug: it is a complex tapestry of ever increasing, dangerous threads that bind you into a self-propagating downwards life style.

I was feeling really worried and apprehensive about doing a detox. This is an extraordinary painful and traumatic process, which nobody wants to do voluntarily. For me this is probably the most significant hurdle. The doctor decided to prescribe Dihydrocodine for me. They don't use it very much nowadays for detoxing unless somebody is allergic to the other medications. They mainly use it for people that need pain relief for backache and symptoms like that.

My drug counsellor and nurse asked what I thought I would need in terms of strength and amount; they always give you the option before prescribing anything. I asked for the slow release tablets as they were the strongest and they would last slightly longer, so I wouldn't need to take so many throughout the day. I also asked for sleeping tablets to get me to sleep. Sleep is usually impossible for the first week and this makes the suffering a lot more intense and difficult. I think the longer you can sleep the less time you have to think about heroin and to feel ill. Personally I wish I could hibernate for a couple of weeks just to get over the worst part of withdrawal symptoms and the craving. I know that personally I find that feeling ill is the worse thing for me. The first few days are the hardest. The mental torture comes afterwards. The more uncomfortable you are, the more you think about using, because you know that the second you take some heroin, then all your suffering will instantly disappear.

I sat at home feeling sweaty, cold and on edge. At this stage, my stomach felt as though it was in knots and I felt like I wanted to be sick. Sometimes, it feels as though there is only so much you can take. I just couldn't sit still and all I could think of was heroin, heroin, heroin. I even said things to my mum, which were very out of character. I began to get even angrier, and even threatened to kill myself. Obviously I wasn't myself. Most people going through a detox are much the same when they have been deprived of their drugs for many hours. I got up and put on some warm clothes because I had goose bumps from head to toe. Strangely, I was sweating at the same time. This is what happens when the heroin leaves your system and your withdrawals are increasing. My legs went from underneath me, but I still struggled to drag myself around and to find anything I needed. Powerful, inner forces were in control of me. I had no idea what I was doing or where I was going or how I was going to get any money. I just knew I had to get out. This behaviour wasn't at all like me, but because I felt so desperate I didn't know what else to do.

My mum was trying to calm me and put me in a positive frame of mind but it just wasn't working. Despite her reassuring words I knew it would take another few days to get over the worst part of this evil and terrible nightmare. I just wanted it to stop, but I didn't want to give up either, and more than anything I just wanted to feel better. So I took some more tablets, like my mum had suggested, hoping that they would take the edge off my suffering. I felt like I was going crazy, but I prayed that the tablets would help. I slipped in and out of consciousness: at least it felt that way, because sometimes I couldn't see the TV and other things around me. I even remember dreaming about having heroin. I tossed and turned in restless turmoil. About ten minutes later I was awake, laying there just thinking of having some gear, wanting that feeling again and knowing that it would make me instantly feel better. I also had an incredibly intense feeling of anxiousness. I was biting my mouth, my feet were twitching, and my legs were aching. Unbelievably I was still intent on going through with the detox. I just had to keep taking my tablets and battle through. My mum was there for me all the way and she kept on telling me how well I was doing. I don't think I was in any frame of mind to appreciate any of this at the time. I survived the first day, and then another, and another.

On this occasion I was able to get through it, because I was only using such a little amount of heroin. It was far from easy, but after the worst three days passed by, I began to feel a little stronger mentally.

It know it doesn't make sense that an addict who goes through such an awful ordeal, can then revert back to heroin again, but you have to understand that heroin is an extraordinary temptation, and I succumbed to it once again and headed down the same old road.

I lived in such a small town it was very hard not to bump into people who were still using, and when you haven't been off heroin for long, you can't help but think of doing it constantly. I needed to get out of the house to get some fresh air and to think about what I was going to do now I was clean, so I took my mum's dog out for a walk. I really wanted to stop using for good, but whatever I tried to do to keep to myself busy and occupied it didn't seem to help. I still had the overwhelming desire for heroin, and it always won.

What had I really become I asked myself? I felt as though I was out of control and a real failure, I felt as though my mind still wasn't completely clear and I even asked God for help, but I was not convinced that even he could help.

Even though I went go to church as a youngster, I still found it hard to believe in something that I wasn't entirely sure about. Even so I still talked to God at times, just in case he really existed, particularly at times when I felt desperately helpless.

Looking back, I suspect that heroin also depletes self-discipline, which would account for my repeated failures. What I really needed was a guardian angel to accompany me day and night to exercise discipline every time I was tempted. The trouble is that such angels are impossible to find.

A BUNGALOW IN CROMER

Paul was still using at the time. His mum also suspected something because we were less than honest about what we were doing. This was mainly because his parents would worry and they would lecture him about it. In some ways Paul was completely irresponsible and would often sink into an almost unconscious 'out of it' state some nights, leaving burn holes in the carpets where he had dropped cigarettes. Another sign was black fingerprints all over the place from the burnt foil. None of this went down very well in such a beautiful house. Weight loss is also something that happens in the matter of weeks after getting back on the gear. This was always a significant indication that Paul was doing heroin, and applied to me too. You lose your appetite and race around so much getting your heroin that you don't leave time to eat. Like I say, the gear comes before anything else. Paul had always been such a fit person over the years when playing football, but now he was gradually deteriorating. A fact, that didn't escape his mum.

We both tried to stop away from each other at times when we were trying to get clean and strong again. We had a tendency to encourage each other to use without realising it. I felt really guilty at times, because my mum and family were trying so hard to help keep me off this awful drug. Paul and I had become very close: I believed I was in love with him, even if people say you don't know what you want at such a young age.

The day came when Paul and I sat down with Cheryl to discuss our addictions, and how it had taken over our lives. We all cried because it got a little heated when Paul asked for more money. It was one of those days when we had no gear and we were extremely ill.

Cheryl had a friend who had a bungalow on the coast, so she planned for us to go there to get away from the town to give us a chance to get clean. Cheryl and Paul's dad Ray were taking us to Cromer, so I said good-bye to my mum and loaded my things into the back of the car. My mum then handed me a small note, which she placed into my luggage bag and told me to think about what she had written.

I decided to leave the note until I got to the place where we were staying because I wanted to read it in private. I just tried to relax on the journey and tried not to think about what was to come next. You might say that we were gluttons for punishment. No sooner do we get clean, and then we slip up and have to repeat the whole process of pain and trauma again.

As we were driving through the winding roads I could see the sea over the hills and I thought this is exactly what I need, some peace and quite and somewhere that is very calming and soothing. We were both feeling quite apprehensive about staying at the bungalow, but it turned out to be absolutely astounding and the view over looking the sea was breath taking.

We had our last bit of gear when we arrived at the bungalow so that it was finished and no longer a temptation. I unpacked and thought maybe we could have a walk along the beach. There were plenty of rooms in the bungalow, so Paul and I stopped in a room that had two beds, because we knew that we would sweat and fidget a lot in the night. That evening Paul didn't fancy a walk, so I thought I would wrap up and have a walk alone. I felt quite emotional that evening, and as I walked along the beach with the sea air hitting my face, I burst into tears. I'm not sure why, maybe it was because of the environment and the circumstances. I just wanted to be happy, but an evil drug had already ruined my life and had taken over everything. I wiped away my tears and decided to walk back in the hope that nobody would notice that I had been crying. I wanted to look strong, not only for myself but also for Paul, and I thought that tears would be taken as a sign of weakness.

That evening we all sat and watched TV and I then got myself to bed, knowing the next day wasn't going to a good day. Paul was the only one who stopped up. He found it very difficult to sleep so he asked his mum if he could have some strong sleeping tablets. The next day I woke early to find Paul staggering around the bungalow in a bit of a state. He had gone over board with the tablets, and when I asked what he had taken he told me ten, which was eight more than he should have taken. His mum was naturally concerned when she woke up, but he told her it was nothing to worry about because he wanted to feel as sleepy as possible, but it just didn't work out that way. During the day Paul fell asleep while I was wide awake. I felt terrible, and all I wanted to do was go home, take some gear, just to take the pain away. This might sound very weak of me to say, but I just couldn't cope and I wanted my mum. I went to the bedroom where Paul was out for the count and took the note that my mum had written to me and began to read it.

Dear Marie,
I know this isn't easy and I know that you will have to go through a difficult time, coming off the drug that has been taking my Marie away from me. I know you can do it, be brave and whenever you want to call me you know you can. Love you darling, love mar.
Xxx

This immediately made me feel guilty that I had just been thinking of myself. It gave me a boost of encouragement all of a sudden. I knew I had to go through it, not just for me, but for my family too.

This was only one of many times that I subjected myself this frightening and painful process. I know we all have choices, but unfortunately my direction was destined to be a tough one. It upsets me, even to this day, that I am not a normal young girl, doing normal things in my life. As I grew up I wanted so much, to be the one who did well at school, to have a goal when I left school, to be a happy young lady who worked hard for what I had achieved, to be an independent normal person just like every body else. I was such a quiet girl, with manners and respect for others, until I stupidly tried drugs, and suddenly I was under its poisonous spell. I looked up to others, and I wanted to make something of myself and possibly to be well known. Instead, I was a weak girl with a lot of issues, a known drugs user with a terrible reputation. To this day I am treated like some kind of alien. I know I have done some horrible things in my life that I cannot forgive myself for. I wish I could turn back the clocks but I know that's impossible, so all I can do is move on. I just wish other people would move on too.

When I returned back home, I knew I needed to keep busy. I visited my dear old Nan and told her that I was trying so hard this time to move forwards with my life. She found it quite hard to understand anything about drugs, but she still tried to listen and give good advice. I loved my Nan for that. She was great at listening, giving advice, and for giving me lots of hugs and kisses.

My Nan was very excited because Lucy, my sister, decided to get married now that she had met the right person. It would great for my Nan to see that Lucy had turned out good. Cheryl also gave me a job at her bridal shop called 'Occasions'. At least I had managed to do one positive thing before I left school, which was to do my work experience at Cheryl's shop. I really enjoyed it even though it wasn't something that I aimed to do in the future, even though I did love anything to do with weddings and maybe even planning them. Working for Cheryl again would be good experience and would improve my confidence and keep me busy.

On my first day at Cheryl's shop there were quite a lot of people coming in and it looked very busy because it wasn't all that big. What the shop lacked in size was made up by the quality and range of lovely dresses.

Even if I say it myself I have good taste and was confident enough to give clients my advice. I really loved pulling dresses out and seeing the excitement on people's faces. I thought that maybe one day, I would have the thrill of planning my own wedding. There were dresses for the brides, bridesmaids, and also at the front of the shop were suits for the mother of the bride. I am sure that Cheryl could see that I really enjoyed my first day. It was very satisfying to be actually doing a job, and it was interesting work because there was always something different to do.

Cheryl asked me to do some window dressing, because she wanted it to look festive, so I went out the back of the shop where there were all different kinds of things that I could dress the window with. I was really proud of what I came up with, and my ingenuity and resourcefulness. I had a good feeling inside me, which I hadn't felt for ages. Heroin is a depressant and has a psychological side effect that also depresses your feelings. Feelings of pride in your work hardly exist, which is why it so surprising that I was felt so positive about keeping my life in order. Paul also began working with his dad and brother, so he was earning some money and attempting to learn more about the trade.

Cheryl asked me if I would like to model some wedding gowns at a fashion show that she was organising at a couple of venues. I had always wanted to do something like modelling and this would be my chance to get dressed up and have an exciting day. I was well aware that most people thought that I was extremely attractive, and heroin ensured that I had the perfect 'skinny' shape for modelling.

The first event was at a place called the Pearls Centre. It was a relatively small gathering of people on this occasion, but from my point of view, it was less daunting. I wore a couple of really expensive dresses and walked down the catwalk, feeling nervous but glamorous at the same time. There were photographers taking pictures and some of the audience also wanted to get snaps of the dresses they liked.

The next event was at a place called Wigston Park and this was a much more laid back event but more exciting because there were lots of girls wanting their pictures taken. I saw the photographer taking pictures of some girls in a horse and carriage, a few minutes later he came over to me and asked me to bend down slightly so my dress was all puffed out and make eye contact with a small child standing next to me with a teddy in her hand. I knew when the picture was taken that it was going to be absolutely gorgeous. I really didn't think at that stage, that he was going to use the photo for the local newspaper, but the next day there it was; such a lovely picture.

The last event was at the Rushdean football club, where the show was staged in one of the big conference rooms there. Paul's dad was chairman of the club and he had his own box when there was a match. When I arrived I was asked if I wanted my hair styling so I went up to the hair salon to get it styled. I wore a dress that was worth a few thousand pounds, and that was a huge sum of money to me. Mind you it wasn't a dress that I would have chosen; it was dark green! I was thrilled about taking part and it is a memory that I will always remember clearly.

Things were going great when Paul and I made a stupid, reckless and irresponsible decision to get some gear one night. We should have realised that you can't just dabble here and there with heroin, particularly if you are an addict. It just doesn't work like that. We were still relatively young and no good at making the right decisions, even though we did questioned if it was or wasn't a good idea. I don't remember how we justified our decision, but we ended up buying some gear with our wages. Obviously we still had a lot to learn.

We became very mellow because heroin is depressant. My brain registered the familiar feeling again: I felt warm and relaxed, began to drift in and out of a light sleep, even though I was still aware of what was going on around me.

When I went home in the evening, my mum noticed that I was full of heroin. I would advise all mothers or parents to keep a close watch on the appearance and behaviour of their children for the signs of heroin use; pinned eyes, itchy skin, sweating, a crease in the forehead from frowning, mood changes and unusual behaviour. People don't realise when they have taken heroin that they stand out like sore thumbs. My mum knew them all, so I tried not to make eye contact but she knew all the same and she was hopping mad. Naturally she wanted to know why I had done it again after being clean for a few months and doing so well. I couldn't give an answer because I had no defence. I just felt terrible that I had let her down once again, and I had let myself down too. I had to make sure I didn't use heroin the next day, but that is much easier said than done.

The whole day at work I couldn't stop thinking about heroin. I even had silly arguments with myself; I know I shouldn't do it, but one more day and that will be it. I know now that it sounds ridiculous; you can't fool yourself. Sadly, addiction robs you your analytical abilities, so you accept such ludicrous reasoning. From then on I was using when I could, and things returned to being the same as they were before.

Paul and I decided to move to a flat in the next village, and his godfather, who owned a holiday estate agents, offered to help us. We were very lucky because it was already furnished and Paul's parents helped with the rest. I was really looking forwards to having our own little place. I was on State Benefit because I wasn't earning enough on the weekends at Cheryl's shop. I think I had £84 pounds to live on for two weeks. The flat was about a seven-minute walk from the main shops and right next to a small post office. I knew I would miss my mum and brother, but at the same time a wanted to be seen as a grown up young woman. Needless to say, neither of us had bothered to do the simple arithmetic to find out if we could afford to live on our own. The fact that we both had expensive drug habits just made matters infinitely worse: but this was better then being homeless or in a shed.

We settled quite well into are new environment, and did exactly what seventeen and nineteen year old kids do; we invited people around and watched lots of TV, and of course smoked our gear. We didn't know anyone in Rushdean so we had to make new friends and it wasn't long before we met the local druggies.

This was a year that I'll never forget, simply because it was such a rotten one. I had no idea that living there would make things a great deal worse. Looking back makes me feel sick thinking about the mess we got ourselves into. Of course we should known it was bound to happen, but we were not in the habit of thinking ahead.

Most days I would wake up feeling miserable and lonely because Paul wouldn't get up until the afternoon, so I was left to mope around by myself. We were attempting to support ourselves and fund our gear at the same time and it lead to a terrible decline in our life style. Some days when we hadn't got money, we went to the shops in High Street and stole whatever we could to sell. It wasn't long before we met people who were prepared to buy the things from us. These 'traders' would give us half price for whatever we could steal.

You are probably thinking 'how could I do such a thing', but we were so desperate. It was choice between making money by stealing, or throwing up violently, sweating buckets, feeling severely depressed and edgy and not eating for days on end. Getting a paid job was not an option; we were unemployable. I'm not proud of myself at all. As I say, I've done some terrible things, but I have never resorted to burglary or robbing an old lady. I suppose I am making excuses because it is only a difference of degree, but what I've done is still enough to stick in my mind with huge regret. This was my journey and one I had a lot to learn on my travels.

Sometimes when we had no cash and I had been up all night pulling my hair out, and seriously withdrawing, I would go out begging at six o'clock in the morning. Typically, I would walk around until I found somebody in the street, and I would ask them in a desperate tone if they could spare a few pounds to get to the hospital because my boyfriend had been rushed in and I had no way of getting there. I assured them that I would post it back if they gave me an address. I told the story with such conviction that it usually worked, although I had to hope they didn't just offer me a lift. No body expected it back, but I would still ask for their addresses just in case. The people I begged from were mostly on their way to work, and had worked hard for their cash, and I was basically stealing it from them, or at least obtaining money by deception. Even now I get embarrassed just thinking about it.

I knew that matters were worse than desperate. My life was gradually falling deep inside a very dark hole, and I wasn't sure that I would be able to climb out again. I was depressed enough already without thoughts like this. There wasn't a day that didn't go by that I cried about how terrible things had got, I felt as though I wanted to be held tight by somebody who could keep me safe from harm, and who loved me. I needed that guardian angel.

LUCY'S WEDDING

Most days I walked around in scruffy jeans that had holes in and an old t-shirt. This isn't my style at all, and my mum always dressed us in very smart clothes. Normally I am proud of my appearance, but while we lived in Rushdean I didn't take care of myself or anything else, and Paul was no better.

It was the week of my sister's wedding and we all needed to get something to wear so my mum picked me up. She didn't mention anything about gear because Lucy and my Nan were in the car as well. We drove to Cheryl's shop to look for a dress for Lucy. I knew that I would be good at finding a dress for Lucy and a suit for Nan. My mum said that my dad had given her some cash to put towards an outfit for me. I immediately felt better knowing I had something nice to wear as well.

I asked Lucy what kind of style was she looking for and pulled out a few. The first was white with pearls all around the top half, and a long flowing skirt. It was the first that Lucy tried on, and straight away I was sure that it was going to look beautiful on her. I got my Nan a chair to sit on because she had severe arthritis in her legs and couldn't stand for too long. While Lucy was in the changing room, I looked for headpieces (crowns) and jewellery that would match the dress. When Lucy emerged, she looked exquisite. She tried a few more dresses, but she was always drawn back to the first.

The next stop was a suit for my Nan. I didn't realise that she had already chosen her suit from a little village nearby. I could see that my Nan was really looking forwards to the wedding: dressed like the queen and watching Lucy walk down the aisle.

At last it was my turn, so we drove to Northampton. Lucy and I had the same sort of taste and she was also very good at finding something that I would like. She picked up a red dress, but I wasn't keen at all, but I loved the second one and the third, and tried them both. I fell in love with the baby blue Chinese silk dress. It was just me. In my excitement I forgot that I didn't have any shoes. In those days my wardrobe was absolutely empty: it didn't exist.

I returned to the flat to find Paul completely 'out of it' as usual. It made me mad to see Paul in that state and not being like it myself, so I grumbled and ask him to 'cook' me up some gear. 'Cook' means putting heroin powder into a spoon with a small amount of citric acid and water and applying heat underneath the spoon. The clear fluid is then drawn into a needle, ready for use. It's a little ritual that you get accustomed to, even though it's not very pleasant. While you are performing this ritual you get a sense of relief and satisfaction in anticipation that you are going to feel much better moments later.

The only food in the cupboards came from Paul's mum. We never had enough cash to buy anything ourselves. Neither of us had the motivation or energy to cook. I know there were times when I felt so hungry I even dreamt of eating food.

Inevitably, Paul and I mixed with the wrong people. We met a guy, called Jay, who came around our flat frequently. At first he seemed harmless enough, but as got to know him it became apparent that he was something else. He was one of the Horn brothers and they were basically 'nut cases', who were always in trouble. One night we went to his tiny bed-sit flat above a chip shop. He was stumbling all over the place and not really making much sense at all, but we thought we would stay for a while just so we didn't look rude. One minute he was talking to us in quite a civilised manner, and then the next minute he just turned as though a switch had been triggered in side his head. We were quite baffled by it all and felt uncomfortable. He was definitely unstable, and not like the person who had visited our flat. He started walking up and down this very small room with his hands on his head, muttering things like he wanted to die. Then he suddenly started on us. We tried calming him down, but it just didn't matter what we said. He was extremely drunk, because I could smell it on his breath when he screamed in my face. When he walked over to the window we took the opportunity to get out of the flat, but he noticed and he asked us both where we were going. I told him that we needed to leave, but he wasn't having any of it and made us sit down while he carried on pacing around the room. This went on for about another ten minutes before the alcohol began to wear off, but it felt like a lifetime. Eventually he fell asleep so we left as quickly as we could. We could not believe that Jay had just held us hostage. You can imagine that we were very relieved to be back home one piece.

It wasn't the only the time Jay lost the plot. Another time when Jay came around our flat was one of those days when we had no money. Jay wanted to get himself some gear, so he sat there counting his money, and because we didn't have any he offered to lend us ten pounds. He just told us to pay him back whenever we could and he left.

We both had a tummy bug and had been throwing up the whole day. We really felt weak and went to bed early in our sleeping bags. Suddenly there was knock on the door. I really didn't want to get up but I found the strength and opened the door. A huge guy barged past me. He went straight over to Paul and begun to knock ten barrels of crap out of him. I was screaming, asking him what Paul had done, and pleaded with him to leave. It seemed like forever that the beating went on, and it wasn't until I said I was going to call the police that he stopped and ran out. I shut the door quickly and looked out of the window to check he had gone, and that is when I saw Jay walking off with him.

I ran to Paul, as he lay there unconscious. I was so scared that I rang for an ambulance. Paul began to come around after about five minutes, but he was in a real bad way. The guy who had done it to him was like a body builder, and Jay had asked him to do that over ten pounds. I told the paramedic what had happened, and he told me I should have rung the police. Calling the police was the last thing we would done, because it would only cause more trouble for us. It wasn't until the next day that Jay came to the door begging us for forgiveness. We just ignored him and he soon went away.

This was one of the many frightening experiences we had in our flat. We were too young and too incapable of sorting ourselves out, quite apart from the problems that heroin brought to our doorstep. It was horrible and I hated living in our own flat. We were too far in trouble to get ourselves out of the mess on our own accord, and we needed help to give us a push, but at the time we didn't listen to the advice of others. I wanted to move back to my mum's house, but I knew that wasn't going to happen in a hurry.

On the day of my sisters wedding I wore my blue Chinese style dress, which was quite short and made me look stick thin. Nevertheless, I actually felt good being able to wear something smart for a change. The Wedding took place at the Perth Hotel in Kettleborough and there were about hundred guests in attendance. My sister and my dad walked up the aisle to her favourite song, 'Your love is my love' by Whitney Houston. It was perfect and she looked stunning in the white pearl dress that I had picked out at Cheryl's shop. My dad looked the proudest dad ever, which made me think to myself that I hope I can do the same, one day.

I tried to enjoy myself, but yet again I was withdrawing from heroin, and my beautiful silk dress showed the sweat marks. It was a real shame because I didn't really feel a part of the wedding. You can tell, because I didn't appear in any of the wedding photos: not one. It was my fault entirely. I had let myself down again because I hadn't even bothered to get my act together for an important family event.

My dad took me back early because I was feeling terrible and needed some gear. Paul didn't even get invited because my dad had always disliked him. In fact he never tried to get to know any of my boyfriends. To be fair, why should he, because all of them were 'druggies'? We arrived at my flat and I looked at my dad and told him I loved him and I missed him. He was quite drunk, and it was the first night ever in my life that I saw a softer side to him. He could see that things were difficult for me, and for once he tried to show some sincere kindness and thoughtfulness.

I told my dad that I needed some money for food and others bits and bobs. I think he really knew what I needed it for deep down because it showed by the look on his face. Normally I would not have asked because there was no chance he would have given me any. He looked worried and guilty, and to my surprise he just burst into tears. I couldn't believe it because my dad had never cried in front of me before, let alone because of me.

I felt quite bad about asking for money, but he handed me a £20 pound note. I felt so bad for taking it, but at the same time I needed it so much. He kind of shrugged it off and said goodbye. I knew it was killing my family to see me in such a bad way, but I was powerless to do anything about it. I couldn't just magic it away.

One day we were both 'clucking' (withdrawing), and we were trying to think of a way we could get some money. Paul had the idea that I should walk down to his godfather's business, just five minutes down the road, and tell him that Paul had a severe throat infection, and he needed some cash to borrow until Paul's mum returned from her holiday. This wasn't actually a lie, but I still felt that I was about to embarrass myself doing this. I think begging and borrowing is a really degrading situation, but when you are desperate you will do anything. I really didn't want to do it, but Paul reassured me and told me that his godfather was a really easy-going guy. We had thought of every other option, so we had no choice.

Paul's godfather bought and sold villas abroad and was a very successful businessman. I walked into the shop, and asked a young guy at the desk if David was in. I felt slightly out of place as I stood there. I told him that I was Paul's girlfriend and he smiled and introduced himself as David's son. His father wasn't in that day so he asked if he could help. I told him the story we had concocted and embellished it to sound more plausible, and he swallowed it. I kind of wished that I had asked for a bit more because it had been so easy. On my way out I told him that the loan would be repaid the second Cheryl returned from holiday.

It didn't occur to me at the time, that whenever we needed to beg or ask for money, it was always me that had to do it. It was always me who had to face the guilt and embarrassment. I was being used and manipulated again just like before.

What was I doing? This was so out of character: it wasn't me, but some person I'd become, I was so ashamed. I walked back as quickly as my sick little legs would take me. I could hardly carry myself I was so weak and thin from lack of food. I wasn't looking after myself at all, and yet strangely I was quite conscious that everything was taking its toll. My body was such a wreck that I hadn't even had a monthly cycle in the past year. Heroin affects most women this way. Heroin had so weakened my motivation and discipline that I no longer cared enough to do anything about it. I lived for the gear everyday and that's all my life revolved around.

When I got back I put on a sad expression. This was something that Paul always did to me, so I thought I would give him a taste of his own medicine. I could see the moment of panic in Paul's eyes and I know I would have been the same if I had been in his shoes. I showed him the money because I didn't want to leave him hanging on any longer. I didn't want to be unkind because he looked quite sick. Every time we managed to get some money it was such a feeling of relief.

A heroin habit is just like having a full time job. It begins by having to scratch around and beg, steal or borrow the money. Now you have to wait for the dealer to switch on his mobile (cell phone) to arrange a place to meet. The next problem is to get a lift to the meeting place. Invariably the dealer will keep you waiting, sometimes for hours. Now you have to get home before you are safe enough to smoke your gear. The day just goes by. It's as if your wristwatch has a hole in it and time leaks out. You can't eat, rest, or talk because your mind is all over the place. You can barely walk depending on how long you haven't used for. This goes on every day, seven days a week with no holidays.

We both knew that we needed to get help, because things were totally out of hand. We said this, countless times, but we never did anything about it, apart from sinking even lower. I never expected my life to go in the direction it had, and I felt completely lost. I was on the verge of walking out in front of a car. At least it would all be over and done with.

As I walked around the corner I bumped in to one of the women who often bought stolen goods from me. She asked if I wanted to get her some things for Christmas to earn myself some money. I told her I would and I would need to know what she wanted. I turned around and was surprised to see my mum's car, and I instantly knew she was there to rescue me from this hideous life style I had fallen into. The relief was unbelievable. My mum ordered me to get in, and she sounded unusually stern and serious.

Out of the blue, my mum had come to save me yet again. She was like an angel that had been sent to me. I was so happy I gave her a big hug. It felt so good to know I still had somebody there who actually cared about me. I know that my desperate situation was self inflicted, but that didn't stop me needing help.

Even though Paul and I were a couple, we rarely showed any affection to one another, because if we weren't sick from not having our gear, we were running around trying to get money to buy more. Heroin was a full-time job with no room for a normal relationship.

My mum could see that I was in a real state but she didn't know about everything that had been going on. I was completely honest and told her everything. She just sat and looked at me with tears in her eyes, but she managed to hold herself together. She put on a brave face that day. I have always admired that about her, and I think I've inherited a lot of my mum's strength. My mum told me why she had distanced herself from me all this time because it made her ill every time she visited at the beginning. I could see the sadness in my mum's face, and she hated to see what was happening to her daughter. I was stick thin, my face was gaunt, and my clothes were filthy and full of holes.

My mum told me a story that day, that when I was a baby, she would take me for a walk in my pram and people would stop to look at me, and tell her how beautiful I was. She said she would walk away and cry with joy, knowing that she had something so beautiful. I could see the pain and the heartache as my mum told me this. It killed me inside, knowing that I was hurting her so much.

My mum asked me very seriously how much I really wanted to get off of heroin and if I was going to put a hundred and one percent into changing my life. She really put things into perspective and everything she said was true. She had said the same thing many times before and it would go in one ear and out of the other. Most youngsters are exactly the same. This time everything hit home; an urgent wake-up call.

Paul and I were both going home and we were both going to get ourselves cleaned up again. Everything had gone on far too long, and we needed that extra help to make it work.

This time I needed a different approach because I had already tried a home detox and going away to the coast in the past. Each and every time, I still came back and slipped into the same terrible nightmare, however much I tried not to. So we had to think long and hard about what the next move was, and we decided that my mum and I would take a week away in Cyprus. Obviously this was probably the best way to get me to stop because I wouldn't be able to find heroin there, but once again it was the problem of how to stop me slipping back when I got home. I would be still vulnerable and not particularly strong after one week, so my mum decided to book me into a London clinic to go for an implant.

An implant contains a blocker that inhibits heroin from reaching the nerve ends. In effect heroin has no effect while the implant is working. This is a very good way to get yourself mentally stronger, as it takes a while to get heroin out of your mind. So the plan was to get straight off the plane after the week away in Cyprus and to go immediately to London to have a Naltrexone implant.

I felt apprehensive and panicky about what this next detox was going to be like, because my mum wasn't sure if I could take some form of medication with me. She told me it would be better to take nothing with me. I needed to be opiate free for at least ten days or more otherwise I couldn't have my implant. I wouldn't be able to take anything else to slowly wean me off heroin. It was going to be extra hard. It was also going to be expensive because the implant alone cost £280 on top of the trip to Cyprus. My mum had a word with my dad and he said he would pay for the implant. This left my mum to pay for the trip and at the time she wasn't earning very much.

It didn't occur to me that unless Paul had something similar planned, the whole enterprise would fall apart when I came back to him. We had a few days to go before the trip to Cypress and I knew I could last that long, so I told my mum that I would need some gear. My mum sat there for a minute, and I could see she wasn't at all happy about the idea, but she knew how I would be suffering, so she took me down the road to a dealer to get some gear. I bought what I would need and went back to the car where my mum told me that she would look after it to make sure I didn't smoke it all.

I didn't really own much apart from a few scruffy clothes that hardly filled the bags I brought back from the flat. My mum was shocked to see that everything I owned either had holes or just looked dirty. She said the first thing we had to do was to buy me some new clothes to take away with me. This was something I just couldn't wait to do: any girl loves shopping. On the first day at home I felt a little uneasy because it was such a dramatic change of life style. No more running around for money and sitting for hours in a dingy cold flat. It felt good to be home, even though I knew there was a crap time ahead of me.

The following morning I woke up and went to the toilet to have my gear and my mum told me to be sure to use plenty of deodorant because she hated the smell after I smoked my heroin. My mum took me to a few shops and we brought some nice outfits to take on the trip. This made me feel tons better.

At the time I was only using from ten to twenty pounds worth of heroin a day, but I knew that I was still going to be very ill, because I was going to have to go 'cold turkey' (doing a detox without supporting medication), and this is the hardest way to detox. I didn't think about this, until I got to Cyprus. Before we boarded the plane I took the last of my heroin so I felt at ease and as comfortable as possible. Without that last dose I probably would not have boarded the plane. I hadn't had any break from heroin for at least a year by this time and I was in for a nasty experience.

DETOX IN CYPRUS

We arrived at Cyprus where we took a coach to the little village of Paphos. I could feel the heat as soon as we got off the coach. I always found that heat and sun made me feel a little better. We were dropped right outside our apartment and we walked around trying to find the reception to check in. At reception we were told our apartment was one floor up, right in the corner near the swimming pool. After unpacking, we went to sit by the pool to enjoy the rest of the sunny day. Later that day I could feel myself becoming more and more irritable and I felt quite ill. I was restless, sweaty one minute and cold the next. I also had an awful tickle in the back of my throat, which was making me reach and sneeze.

I didn't want my mum to stop inside to look after me all the time, because it would ruin her holiday too. In my eyes, I wanted her to enjoy her ten days, as I knew she never had much time off work to relax and unwind. I tried my hardest to keep busy, restlessly going outside for a short while, then went back inside again. My mum kept calling in to check that I was all right because she was so concerned. I was struggling to drink, because I could easily dehydrate in the heat, besides I needed to drink more to flush all the rubbish out of my body. I was determined to get well and to enjoy the last days of our time away, at least.

That night was dreadful. My stomach was incredibly painful and I was having all the same symptoms as earlier in the evening, but a lot worse. At one point because I couldn't get settled, I went into the shower, sat on the floor and just let the water run down on me. This helped to relax me for a short while and I came out to lay on the bed with towels wrapped around me. I didn't have the energy to even dry myself.

My mum woke up very early to see I me sitting there biting my lip anxiously. I told her that I needed some sleeping tablets, because without sleep it was making things worse. All I wanted to do was sleep this nightmare away, but that's the last thing that happened. So my mum went out to the chemist and returned with a little box in her hand, which turned out to be Nytol. Bless her, she tried her hardest, but they wouldn't give her anything stronger over the counter. In desperation, I ended up taking the whole box of Nytol, and still didn't sleep a wink. What a surprise! Take it from me herbal sleeping remedies don't work if you are coming off a very strong drug. There are only a couple of strong sedatives that work, and they are only available on prescription from a qualified drug worker, or a doctor.

In Cypress I experienced a very difficult ordeal, and each day I would hope and pray that I would begin to feel a little better. Eventually I did, and I was able to do some sun bathing in the last couple of days of our holiday. I wanted to celebrate my progress, so my mum and I went for a drink to a bars that was about five minutes walk from the apartment. I still felt sweaty and not completely myself, but I could handle it. I walked in feeling a little uneasy, nervous and fidgety. My mum brought us both a couple of drinks and after a short while I began to relax and not worry about whether people were looking at me or not. In my case, I have a tendency to feel paranoid when coming off the gear, probably because I am out of my comfort zone.

The bar was decorated to look like an English pub, and I later found out that two young English guys owned the bar. The place began to fill with people and we sat at the bar minding our business, when a young guy came over and offered to buy me a drink. I was quite surprised because I wasn't looking particularly glamorous, although the sun had given me a bit of colour so I looked much better than I actually felt. At first, I had no idea that this very attractive young man was chatting me up. He stood speaking to my mum and I for a short while and then told us he had to go to meet some friends, and he asked if I would like to meet up the next day. I thought that there was no harm in two people having a quite drink together.

I had a real good think about things that night as I lay in bed. I thought that Paul and I should have a break from one another if I was to stay clean. We had been through a lot and it hadn't been a particularly good relationship because of the gear, but I knew we would always stay friends. Paul and I had some really bad arguments during the time we were together, and it was always about that rubbish. It was a shame, because we had gone from being a very nice looking, decent couple, to a complete mess.

Anyway, I decided to meet with this guy called Matthew the next day, which pleased my mum. I was feeling slightly better than the day before and I tried to make myself look as good as I could, because I had a real complex about being so thin and gaunt.

Matthew and I sat chatting most of the evening because I am not really a drinker. It only takes a few glasses to make me quite tipsy. I hadn't asked what kind of work Matthew did, because I knew he would then ask what I did. I always struggled when people asked me questions like that. What could I tell them? I could only lie and say that I was at college, or I was still deciding what I wanted to do for a future career.

Well, he asked me to guess what work I thought he did. He told me he was 26 years old and that he was a northerner. I had no idea, but I guessed at a few jobs like, a sales rep or estate agent, because he came across as very chatty. He didn't have hard working hands like a mechanic or labourer. In the end I ran out of ideas so he told me that he was a policeman. I nearly choked on my drink. I couldn't believe that a 'copper' (policeman) had been chatting me up. I mean it just shows that you can't judge people by appearances. To him, I was just a normal girl, and it really felt great.

Later that evening I went back to his apartment to continue our chat because I really enjoyed the company of this normal guy who had lots to talk about, which was such a welcome change. Paul and I rarely had much to talk about, because of our crazy life style. In the end I fell asleep on the little sofa in his apartment. I woke up with severe stomachache and crept to the toilet. I was so embarrassed when I had to wake Matthew to ask him to pay for a taxi back to my apartment. The poor guy must have realised afterwards why I rushed off. It wasn't the aroma of my perfume that I left behind in his toilet.

Looking back, it strikes me as bizarre, that a few weeks before going to Cyprus I was a total wreck, and a few days later I was being chatted up by a police officer.

I regretted drinking the night before because the following day I spent most of my time on the toilet. I was still going through my detox and I was probably trying too hard to fit in again and this resulted in me feeling unwell again. I've never been one to drink much alcohol. It puts me off when I see people acting aggressively after drinking too much. I hated it as a child.

Maybe I am paranoid, but I always get annoyed when people presume that heroin addicts all look the same. It just isn't true. Not all addicts look like scumbags. Addicts come from any class and any background: heroin isn't picky.

Immediately after we left the airport on our return from Cyprus, we had to dash to the Stapleford Clinic in London. I felt quite apprehensive but at the same time really positive about trying something new, that might help me mentally to keep clean. The lady at the desk told us that we would have to wait for a short while because there was a queue in front, so we went for a drink in a small coffee shop just down the road. My mum and I talked about the implant procedure and then before I knew it was time to go back. By this time I felt butterflies in my stomach and I begun to sweat with worry. We sat in the small waiting area for a short while before I was called into a large room where Dr Brewer introduced himself. He asked me to sit down so he could explain about the implant procedure. He said that I would have a few injections around the groin area to make it numb so that he could then make a small incision to insert the implant. I asked if it was going to hurt much and he told me that there would only be a few needle pricks.

While I was waiting in the chair I was looking around the room where I was sitting. There were lots of pictures of the human body and also a framed certificate. The doctor told me that he normally treated people for drug and alcohol abuse but recently he had also just begun to give treatment and psychiatric help to sex addicts. I thought that was quite funny at the time, because I had never heard of people needing treatment for too much sex.

He then asked me to lie on to the operating table where I had to pull my jeans down as far as possible so he could get to the groin area. I know that he was a doctor, but I still felt enormously embarrassed, and I was totally petrified about what he was going to do next. He put on gloves and then disinfected the area where he intended making the incision. He even asked me if I wanted to look, but I felt squeamish about that so I carried on looking at the wall where all the pictures and structures of the human body were. Dr Brewer then used a blue pen to mark the incision for the implant. I then saw him selecting the needle from his little metal table where there were lots of different instruments. When I saw the size of the needle I was petrified. I know this sounds very bizarre, because I had injected myself with heroin many times, but this was entirely different. I knew that I was going to feel the pain of the needle and that it wouldn't be accompanied by my usual heroin reward. It was much more painful than I expected, because I could feel him moving the needle around, and it made me feel sick. I remember holding my mum's hand so tightly that she must have lost all feeling in it.

He then left me for few seconds to allow the anaesthetic time to work. There was no doubt that it was working because I couldn't feel my lower half at all. It was very odd because I knew I wouldn't feel the pain of the incision, it was just the thought of cutting my skin that worried me. I couldn't help getting a glimpse of what he was doing, and it looked dreadful. He had to hold the skin with an implement whilst forcing the implant in and then pushing it down into place. It was horrible and the whole time I could feel him pulling and pushing the skin. The implant itself was about as big as four long paracetamol tablets, and after it was all finished I could clearly see it beneath the skin. At last I could face the world knowing that I was protected and immune to heroin.

I was very lucky that my family paid for this treatment, because I know a lot of drug users wouldn't be able to find this kind of money. Most users will never have the opportunity that I had. It takes at least two years fully to recover from the mental and physical effects of heroin addiction, which accounts for so many addicts returning to that evil road to destruction. At least I had the implant to support and help me escape that dreadful life. I felt so positive about making good.

I was thinking about going to college to do counselling. I mean you can't get a better counsellor, than somebody who has experienced drug addiction. I knew what it was like and I really wanted to help other people to avoid making the same mistakes as I had. So I tried to find out about college courses like a qualification in Health and Social Care. I was really excited about doing something positive, and it was just what I needed to keep myself busy. However, when I tried to get myself booked in for the next course I found out that I couldn't go on a course because I had been on drugs, and I needed to have been off the drug list for at least ten years, before I could do a job that involved contact with the public. I couldn't believe what I was hearing, and it really put me down. Once again heroin was ruining my chances. I had escaped its clutches, but it was still hanging on like grim death.

Unfortunately, when my implant ran out I had another slip up. I suppose this is a good indication how much I needed the support of Naltrexone to keep me clean. Obviously I needed another implant before my habit got any worse. In the meantime I got a prescription for Naltrexone tablets to keep me safe until the next implant. I had only been using for about three weeks but I still needed to detox before taking the tablets. My plan was to do a few days without and then start the tablets. This wasn't really a good idea because the official advice is to go at least ten days without, before taking Naltrexone. On reflection, I think our family had a dangerously cavalier attitude towards medication of any sort, which you will have gathered from this book so far, and we often ignored medical advice in favour of our own diagnosis and judgement. In my particular case I had frequently taken recreational drugs regardless of medical dosage. It was only a matter of time before our ignorance would lead to near tragedy.

I was about to go to my dad's place for the day, but before I went my mum gave me a half tablet of Naltrexone. By the time I had got to my father's house, I was bent over in agony and had to run to the toilet. I thought I was dying. I couldn't make out what was wrong with me, until it dawned that the tablet might be reacting with me. I was right. I still had residual opiates in my system and the Naltrexone was doing exactly what it was designed to do.

My dad didn't know how to cope with the situation. As it happened Paul called me, so my dad dropped me at Paul's house even though he didn't like Paul. Perhaps my dad thought that Paul might know how to handle the situation. By this time, Paul's mum and dad had moved to a little village nearby because they couldn't stand living in our little town. It had so many bad memories for the whole family. When I arrived at the house I could barely stand. I was leaking from every orifice, which was an extremely unpleasant experience. It was worse than any illness that I had ever had in my whole life.

Despite these horrific side effects, my mum carried on giving me Naltrexone without me knowing. I also suffered dramatic weight loss and I could barely move for another week afterwards. My body felt as though it had been run over by a bus. My features were drawn like a corpse, and I lost my appetite. None of us really knew the implications of taking Naltrexone too soon. Be warned, read the instructions before messing with self-administered medication. I know from bitter experience that it can be dangerous.

I have a friend who actually had a stroke from having an implant and not being completely clear of opiates. I think they are supposed to give a urine test to check for any opiates prior to inserting an implant. I slowly recovered and was taken care of by my one and only friend Paul. We basically nursed one another through this traumatic time.

I had another two implants just to be on the safe side, and this was the first year I can actually say was one of the best years of my life. I didn't get my self away from drugs totally, but I made new friends and began to live again. I was still living at home and I loved it. In the mornings I actually woke up feeling like I was full of life, energy and personality. I regained myself; Marie came back to life again. I was almost back to being a normal everyday eighteen year old. My social skills weren't great because my life style had been centred on drugs and nothing else, so I really needed to find my feet again in this first year.

BILLY

This was a better year, because I was clean, but in some ways life wasn't as good as I had hoped for. I had missed so much when I was on autopilot on heroin, and now I felt as though I needed to catch up with everyone else. My mum keep telling me that I should stop panicking and that everything would come in time, but I couldn't help wanting things to happen sooner. Some days I felt really down and fed up. I had a wide circle of friends, which was a first for me. A few of the girls were bisexual or lesbians, but this didn't worry me. Their preferences were their choice and it was not up to me to judge. I knew exactly where my preferences were.

As time went on people started to accept me again, and actually spoke to me. I have never been able to fathom why some people only speak to me when I am clean? Why am I any different if I am on drugs? As far as I am concerned I have an illness, so I need support and encouragement: not negative attitudes. I suppose it is like racism: there is no logic to bigotry.

I began to experience all the normal feelings that everybody gets, and it was brilliant. I had missed it for such a long time. Going shopping for new clothes made me feel good, and having someone whistle at me on the street gave me a boost. Even being able to earn my own money was unusually satisfying. All these things were coming back to me, because I had forgotten for a while how great life really was. I appreciated every minute of it. We sometimes take things for granted, but if we step back and realise that we could be in a lot worse position. We need to recognise that there are a lot of people in this world who are in a lot more trouble than ourselves.

It took me a while to feel mentally strong enough to go out and find myself work because I suffered from panic attacks when I was in a busy environment. If I stepped outside my comfort zone, I found it hard for a while to get use to 'normal' everyday activities. Previously I had been entirely dependant on heroin, and now I was no longer able to use it like a crutch to lean on. Things don't seem to bother you quite as much when you are on heroin, because it blocks your emotions and the way you think about things. Now that my mind was clear and I could see everything much more clearly, I even noticed small things that I hadn't notice before. I had been living in a heroin bubble, so I wasn't aware of much of what was going on around me.

Life had started to get so much better now, but it was still very difficult to adjust to normality. I was taking each day as it came, and used all my strength to try and make some good out of it. I started going out more and socialising, because this was something that I hadn't done in a very long time. I discovered that a having a drink elevated my confidence. The alcohol helped boost what heroin had suppressed for so long; my personality and confidence. Even though I had seen people behave in such abusive and aggressive ways when they had drink, I still had that inner need to fit in with the crowd to make me feel I was as good as anybody else.

Almost everyone at the time was using recreational drugs, pills (ecstasy), base (amphetamine), ketamine (horse tranquilliser) and MDMA. I certainly don't recommend that anyone uses drugs to have a good time, but I will be entirely honest that I really enjoyed my time out with my friends. This sounds very bizarre, but I was actually more scared about using ecstasy than when I was using heroin. I had heard stories that people had died from using pills or had bad reactions, so I worried about taking them each and every time I used them. With heroin, I knew where I was and knew how to avoid the risks, although there was always a risk of over-dosing when injecting.

You could argue that I was careless in my choice of friends, because I had effectively switched from one group of drug users to another. I certainly didn't do this on purpose. Statistically, less than 20 percent of my age group experimented with drugs, so I suppose I was unfortunate to find groups where drug taking was so prevalent.

We often went out to clubs, but mainly ones that played music like 'hardhouse' and 'drum and base'. My love of music was awakened about this time, when I was eighteen, and I saw music in a totally different light. I also had my eyes on one particular guy in our group called Billy, who went to school with Paul when they attended a private school in Wellington. I had really come to an end with Paul and wanted a fresh start altogether. Most of all, I was worried that I would never be accepted by another guy, particularly one who had never used heroin.

Strangely, other drug users would look down on heroin users as if they were the lowest of the low, and referred to us as 'smack-heads'. How they could be so hypocritical defeats me to this day.

As soon as Billy took some interest in me, I really fell for him in a big way. Paul was instantly relegated as a 'has been' although I didn't actually tell him so. One evening Paul came around to my house when I wasn't there, and my mum told him the truth. I couldn't believe she would do such a thing, but I had been very selfish and worried about how to break the news to him. I didn't want to hurt him, but my mind was made up; I wanted to be with Billy. When I arrived home I knew straight away that 'do-do' had hit the fan when my mum told me what she done. I ran out of the house before Paul could say anything, and headed towards the phone box with Paul running after me, begging me not to leave him. It was horrible hearing him cry. He sounded so broken hearted, but it was really for the best for both of us. At the time he couldn't see it like that. Paul eventually got the message that I wasn't going to speak to him, so he walked away and I did the same.

I wanted to see Billy because I couldn't really cope with what had just happened. I knew that I'd hurt Paul so much. I loved Paul to bits as a friend, but no longer as a boyfriend. The last thing I wanted was to hurt him. I lost Paul's friendship for some time afterwards, which was really hard for me. We both went our separate ways and fortunately it did turn out for the best.

I began to find myself again, and I felt so happy. I had a boyfriend who really loved me and I had a great group of friends. It was all coming together nicely, and it was heavenly to wake up every morning feeling good, with the day ahead of me.

When the weekends came around I was always out partying. Ecstasy was quite a different drug became it made everybody seem so happy and lovable. This was so different though from heroin. Obviously, after a couple of heavy nights out I needed to 'come down' (recover). I had a really good time mostly, but I will be honest and tell you that the after effects are not healthy. You feel so rotten for the next few days, and sometimes it makes you feel quite down in the dumps depending on what you have taken.

I went to a club called 'Storm' quite a lot. We would all go out dressed up in fluorescent clothing and my hair done in little buns, with spiked bits coming out of them. I thought that I looked wicked at the time (cool). It was great fun, and exciting, knowing we were all going out to have a great time. We would dance, and then sit down where ever we could, and just start randomly chatting to anyone and everyone sitting next to us. That is what pills do. In our local slang we called it 'in a bit of a pickle' or being 'struddled'. You probably see it as sounding totally crazy, but to all of us being insane and crazy seemed hilarious at the time. Some people could handle their drugs whereas some couldn't and would get themselves into a real mess. For some reason, it really shows with some people when they have taken ecstasy, because they begin to gurn (make strange faces), their chins are all over the place.

These drugs make you feel immensely high for many hours, and this is followed by a period of feeling equally low. At the time I could only see the funny side to taking these drugs, but I know now that they can also be so dangerous and there are many more bad sides than good. In fact I am sure that a lot of my anxiety is down to taking drugs over the past. This is a legacy that reminds me of my stupidity. Take my word for it: you can't beat feeling high naturally without drugs.

I got myself a job in a warehouse, which is not something I really wanted to do but I needed to start somewhere. It was with an agency so the money wasn't so great, but what I was mainly looking forwards to was a regular wage at long last. I found it easy though, picking and packing, it wasn't a job where I had to use my brain, but after my hectic weekends, this was just as well.

Billy worked in computers and had a very well paid job and owned his own car. We would spend time with each other after work, which was nice because we had something to look forwards to after work. I had been in a serious relationship with Billy for about ten months and then suddenly I became a different person now that we had been together for so long. My moods were very up and down at the time, and even now I am still quite ashamed how I treated people. I had no idea why I was so grumpy and short tempered. One day, on my day off from work my mum told me to get up because we were going down the chemist to get a pregnancy test. This was the first that I had heard my mum say such things and this startled me. It really hadn't crossed my mind. I have to admit that she had frequently remarked about my difference in weight and my moods but I didn't take much notice.

I lay there with my mind working over time. Maybe I was pregnant because I hadn't used precautions when I was with Billy. I must have been stupid to think it wouldn't happen to me. My mum bought a pregnancy test kit for me and I did the test. The look of fright on my face must have said it all. I was pregnant. The first thing my mum told me was that I should think very carefully before making any decisions. I needed to be absolutely certain I was ready to have a baby. I knew she was right.

The first thing I did was to tell Billy as soon as I got home and he was very calm like he always was. Like me, I don't think he was ready for a child either. I didn't know what I wanted. I hadn't yet told my Nan, because I didn't want to, until I knew exactly what I was going to do. I told my mum not to say anything to anyone because I didn't want people judging me one way or the other. I didn't know that my mum had already told my Nan. She always went to my Nan when she was worried about something or a member of the family.

I wasn't ready for a baby, but at the same time when I felt my stomach and thought there is a living being in my tummy. What should I do? I had no idea how far gone I was, because I still had my monthly cycle. In fact I had only missed one period, and that's why it hadn't crossed my mind that I might be pregnant. I had to wait a couple of weeks until I could go for a scan, and I asked Billy if he would come with me, so he booked a morning off from work.

On the day of the scan my head was all over the place. I was feeling so guilty because of all the drugs I'd been putting into my body whilst I was pregnant. I felt so selfish and sick with guilt. This made me wonder if the baby would be healthy if I was to go through with the pregnancy. In the waiting area there were lots of heavily pregnant ladies and this made me feel very motherly. I was clearly still in two minds. I found it so difficult. I knew I'd messed up so much up already over the years and I was thinking that this is supposed to be a magical time, an exciting time for a couple, and obviously I didn't feel like that one bit. Instead I felt worried, scared and totally confused.

I was called into the room for the scan, and Billy came in with me. I was both apprehensive and intrigued. I wanted to know how far gone I was into my pregnancy. I looked on the screen, as the nurse turned it away, and when I saw this tiny little baby with a little heartbeat, I burst into floods of tears. The nurse looked really shocked by the way I reacted.

The nurse told me that I was twelve and a half weeks gone, and that I should speak to a counsellor about what I intended to do next. To be honest I couldn't take anything in as I sat in the small waiting room because my mind was a complete wreck. A lady came in and sat down. She seemed very polite and spoke very quietly. She explained that if I decided on a termination that it wouldn't be a normal termination. All the rest was a blur.

My mind was working over time and I needed time to think about it all. At the same time, I realised that there was an urgent time limit, and I needed to make my mind up exceedingly quickly. When I messed up, I messed up good and made a professional mess of things. I went away in a state of shock. I was a very mixed up young lady who had previously made some extremely bad decisions in my life so I really wanted to think this one over properly. Unfortunately Nature herself was pressuring me to make a quick decision. Another week went by and I was beginning to show and feel the baby in my stomach. I was having flutters and this added to my difficulties.

I lay in bed crying. Billy and I weren't getting on as well as we had been, or to be more precise, I couldn't make out what I wanted out of the relationship. I had a vision that I was making a huge mess of things all over again and I felt so stupid. As I write this I can't help crying and feeling a sense of pain and guilt. My advice to all teenagers is not to fall pregnant. The decisions will break your heart either way, just like it did to me.

The worse thing about it was that my Nan knew about it. She could never have children of her own, which is why she adopted my mum and her brother. Shortly after that, my Nan passed away, which was a huge shock.

I went to work as usual at the warehouse and unexpectedly got a message from my manager saying my mum had called and she was going to collect me after work. It was most unusual, but I didn't think much more about it until I saw a very sad look on her face as she sat in the car. Immediately I knew that something wrong when my mum burst into tears and finally told me that my Nan had passed away a couple of hours ago.

My mum was obviously distraught, and I just couldn't believe what had happened because she seemed fine only two days previously. We made our way around to my Nan's flat. When I walked in my sister was there already. She was hysterical, which I didn't expect at all. I went into the small kitchen where my Nan lay. She looked so peaceful, just as though an angel had laid her out perfectly. I held her ice-cold hand and I remembered what she had told me once as a child when we spoke about dying. She told me that we go to heaven, so I asked her if she could help me with my homework if she died, and she replied that she would have a good go at helping me and laughed. The main thing that stuck in my head was that she told me to celebrate her life and not to cry. She didn't want us to be upset by her loss, but rather we should feel happy to have known her and loved her. Despite her wishes: her loss devastated me.

It took me quite some time to grieve, but my Nan was the first person I had lost, and it reminded me that she wasn't going to be the last.

I felt as though I put extra worry on my Nan and that I might have been partly responsible for her death, even though my family have always said otherwise. I loved my Nan so much, and I'd lost her, and I also had a baby that was going to be terminated too. It was a really bad time for all of the family, and to this day I always speak to my Nan when times are bad and I miss her. She will always be in my heart.

It wasn't long after that my date came through for my termination. This wasn't going to be a normal termination: I was going to be induced, but had no idea how awful it really was going to be.

I started a different job not long after that traumatic time. I was so excited and felt a big sense of achievement. My sister, Lucy dropped me at the interview as it was in her hometown. The job was working for an estate agent, where I would be trained and to work as an administrator. I wasn't very confident about getting a job like that, but they later said that I spoke so clearly, and I came across so positively that they called me as I walked down the street five minutes later to tell me I had the job.

My sister collected me, and she could see how overjoyed I was. I was really keeping my fingers crossed that this could lead me to a decent career ahead of me. Billy and I split up not long before I started at my new job. It was partly because of my terrible moods and the confusion after bumping into Paul again. What eighteen-year old girl really knows exactly what she wants out of life? I certainly didn't. It didn't take me long to find my feet at my job. To be honest, it wasn't how I imagined it would be. I felt I was doing all the boring jobs, and I knew that I had a lot more to give.

Although I had only been at the firm for a couple of months and barely knew anybody, I was going to the Christmas party that was being held at a club. You always get one who isn't particularly nice in the work place. There was one girl that just didn't seem to want to get to know me or to be friendly whatsoever. In my paranoid stupidity, I always took this sort of thing as a personal snub, instead of rising above it and ignoring the person.

The Christmas party went well. It was another opportunity to dress up and try and be a normal person. It really felt good because nobody knew about my past, so I was treated like any other person would be. I think I hadn't really dealt with the death of my Nan and my abortion because there were days when I just sobbed and felt ever so low. I should have had counselling to get over my Nan and for the abortion. I also missed Billy but I still thought I wanted a relationship again with Paul. Looking back, I must have been mad. I suppose everybody makes the wrong choices at times.

I should have stayed single and concentrate on my new job, but Marie didn't do things quite that way unfortunately. Not only did I have a knack of making big mistakes, but I also managed to make a full disaster of it.

THE MUSICIAN

Christmas had just gone and I had been out with a group of friends, so I was feeling really tired, and more than likely on a 'comedown' from stimulant drugs. Paul called me and I decided I really wanted to see him. He was with another friend, Lee the musician. Lee and I had been friends since I met Mick, my first boyfriend. Apparently Lee tried to chat me up, but Mick warned him off by saying I was far too young. That's when Mick made his move and I most definitely ended up with the wrong guy, he destroyed my youth and me as a person.

I met Paul and Lee and we went for a walk to the lakes in the little village where Lee lived. We sat around chatting when Paul got some gear out and started to smoke it. I waved away the smoke and complained angrily that it stunk. A second later, in a moment of total madness, stupidity and lack of self-control, I took the tube from Paul's hand and began to inhale the fumes. There it was, that special feeling again: the feeling of warmth, the feeling of relaxation and of no cares. My 'comedown' had gone and I started to gouch (close my eyes). I sat on the little wooden bench in the bird watch shed by the lake and I was completely 'out of it' once again. What had I done? In a moment of madness I had ruined a whole year of hard work staying off the gear. It is true that I had taken other drugs, but I think I would have grown tired of them with time.

You must know what is coming next. I soon became addicted again, and lost my job because I couldn't make it in some days. If I had no gear then I couldn't go to work as I felt ill and was unable to face anybody. Without work I would have no money to get my gear. Without gear I couldn't work. It was an endless, vicious cycle. I failed once again. I was a walking, unreliable disaster. As usual, the magnitude of the disaster would get much worse.

My mum soon realised that I was back on heroin again. To this day I regret putting my Mum through all this grief again. It was the last straw for her. She had another relationship after Andy, and she really loved this guy. He was with my Mum for about two years, when he suddenly decided to go off with another woman. My Mum took it hard. Not long after that he got stomach cancer and died within a week. It really did upset her, so she didn't need me to add to her troubles after all her bad luck. I think deep down she thought they might have got back together at some stage, but then he passed away and this really affected her.

Paul and I didn't last long after that and it was really for the best. I then started going around the local doss houses again taking heroin. In the old days these houses would probably have been called opium dens. For the most part they were just ordinary houses where heroin users would congregate to inject or smoke their gear. I wasn't using for long, but it was long enough for me to have to go through a detox all over again. You might be thinking that this girl must be some sort of masochist, who enjoys the self-inflicted pain of doing a detox. The truth is that the very thought of doing a detox scares the crap out of me.

I began to see Lee after a few months and we spent a lot of time together. It started when he sent me quite a flirtatious message. I always thought he was quite sweet and things started to escalate from there. We had always been close, and I use to go out with him in his car in the early days, when Mick was in prison. He was a very quiet, shy person, but he always felt he could speak to me. Our history stretched back to the first time we met at the Friday night football club discos. This time, I thought that I had found my best friend for life. It was a completely different relationship to those I had been in previously, but it was just right. There was no arguing and we had quite a bit in common, we were both so easy going.

After my slip-up back down the path of heroin, my dad and I spoke about me having another implant, which I knew was the only thing that gave me extra support after detoxing. My mum told me I needed to stay with my father for a week or so to get myself cleaned up again. This wasn't an option I wanted, but I had no other choice. My dad has always found it very difficult over the years to understand my addiction and how extremely difficult it is to do a detox. I had only been 'using' for a couple of months, but I needed to get back to how I was during the year when I was clean. I had my own room at my dad's house and I spent quite a bit of time lounging about because I wasn't feeling well at all. My dad made sure there was no way I would get out to get any gear. At one point I even thought about jumping out of the window onto a plastic ledge, but knew it was far too risky because I would have hurt myself for sure.

Lee and I tried to arrange to detox at the same time, but I would have a head start on him because my implant operation occurred before the date set for Lee to have his implant. Lee and I had been on heroin nearly as long as each other. He was one of the earlier ones in our town.

Yet again I found myself travelling down a well-trodden path down to London to an implant clinic. This time, my father and some friends of his took me. I remember the day quite clearly. It was coming up to Christmas and I remember London being very busy as we caught the underground and then walked along to Eccleston Street. I was still not feeling too great that day, as we rushed to get to the clinic. My Dad and I joked with one another as we sat in the waiting area. He was always one to make a joke at a tense time. I will never forget when I was ten years old; he sat and held my hand at the dentist's, trying to keep my mind off of having four teeth out. He was a pillar of strength for me then, just as he was now at the clinic. He was so sensitive on this occasion. These are memories that I will hold onto forever.

The implant clinic had moved across the road, which didn't really matter, and this time a different doctor carried out the implant operation. He was a foreign doctor, so I made conversation and asked what country he came from. I recall him saying Sweden. I explained that this was my fourth implant before he started the operation. I had already had three implants so he needed to decide where would be best to put the fourth implant, as both the left and right side of my abdomen had scar tissue. I felt a little uneasy when he told me he had only been doing implants for six months. I prayed that nothing would go wrong. My Dad watched and still made jokes as I was having the nasty bit done with the anaesthetic injection.

After the operation my Dad's friends wanted to have a look round London. I had just had surgery so all I wanted to do was get back home as soon as possible. Instead, the crowds doing their Christmas shopping were jostling me. I felt tired and wanted to rest. My Dad was getting irritated, because I wasn't keeping up, and I wasn't being particularly talkative. I was in pain as the local anaesthetic started to wear off and I was on the point of tears. It seemed to me that my Dad and his friends didn't care how I felt. The day was turning into a nightmare. I wanted it over and done with so I could get back home. I think my Dad just didn't want to feel embarrassed, and this was one of those times when he only thought of himself, rather than my welfare.

I moved in with Lee at his mum's house. His room was typically boyish and in desperate need of a makeover before it would look anything like a home for me. We went out and bought some wallpaper and paint, and began redecorating the room. Yellow and blue didn't seem too girly to me, and Lee didn't object. We ripped up the carpets and luckily there were polished floorboards underneath, so that made life a lot easier. We obviously didn't have enough money for a new carpet. Lee and his mother went out shopping one day, and they came back with a surprise; they had ordered a double bed, which would be much more comfortable than the single bed we had been sharing. Two in a single bed is a recipe for backache.

I had started to get accustomed to my implant by this time, but Lee still needed cleaning up. For a while after the implant I was living the life of a heroin addict, but without actually being on heroin. It was extremely difficult for me to see somebody close to me, going through the daily routine of an addict. I got to see what it was like from the other side of the fence. I found it very, very stressful and upsetting at times. This was the first insight I had of the pain and suffering my parents experienced. It was horrible. It was probably a little harder for me because I still had physical and mental cravings, which would last for a long time yet. I even went with Lee to score (buy heroin). To be fair, Lee tried not to smoke heroin around me, but sometimes that was quite difficult.

This routine went on for a few weeks, and by then I felt a wreck. The worry and stress of watching someone using was getting me down. I was getting a daily dose of what my parents had been through. I really feel for anyone that isn't on heroin, but has to live around people who are. It is an extremely stressful situation for anyone. My advice would be to avoid this situation unless you are very strong willed with nerves of steel. I wasn't either of these things, so I found it very tough going. I should have stepped back a few paces for a while just until Lee was off the heroin, for my own sanity.

I wanted to help Lee get clean, which was a task and a half, but I wanted more than anything for both of us to get our lives together. He was extremely sick. I thought that I suffered while doing a detox, but it looked as if it was a hundred times worse for poor Lee. Maybe because he was slightly older and has always done such a lot of heroin. Each and every person reacts differently to doing a detox. He finally began to feel a little better after about a week. I encouraged him to try and get up, to have a bath and to try and eat. I think it helped him knowing I was there to push him all the way.

Lee had his implant not long afterwards, and for the first eight days after his operation he was violently sick, over and over again, bringing up bile and any food or drink that had consumed. Lee always suffered an extreme reaction to implants, and this was the second time he had to endure eight days of severe sickness following the surgery. He lost about a quarter of his body weight, which made him very weak physically. It is very difficult to watch this happening to somebody that you really care for. I even had a few moments where I went to the bathroom to cry.

It wasn't for at least a month afterwards that Lee and I began to live a little, as we were now both clean again. We had a great time; going out, shopping, taking more interest in music, and I even started driving lessons again, which my Dad had bought me as a birthday present. I don't think I was sufficiently organised enough to match the lessons with the theory test and the practical driving test itself. Whatever the reason, I didn't finish the lessons. I was nineteen years of age and had no driving licence.

I had another slip up shortly after my implant run out. I call it a lapse not a relapse, I only used a couple of times and something happened that made me realise I was making a huge mistake. I went out with one of my old acquaintances in his convertible car, while Lee was out swimming one day. We picked up Paul and then went to Rushdean to score some gear. You are probably ahead of the story here, because the combination of Paul and gear can only mean one thing. Would I ever learn? When we arrived at the dealer's house, he came out and I could see he was showing off as he was flashing a huge amount of gear. After serving us up (selling to us), he kept the gear on him and asked for a lift to his mate's house. Paul commented that he must be mad to bring out his whole parcel (all his gear). Anyway, we all jumped into the car and we drove down into the main High Street.

Before we knew it we had the police behind us in a plain car. The first we knew they were on our tail was when they put the blue light on to catch our attention. We all panicked. The dealer stood up in the open top convertible car and threw his gear away. I put mine in my waistband, and Paul hid his down the back of the seat.

The police grabbed the dealer because they obviously saw the gear fly through the air into the back of a house. They could hardly miss it, because it was as big as a tennis ball. A policewoman came over to me and asked me to empty my handbag. I have to confess that I was on the verge of messing my pants at this point, as she started to search my bag. Paul was also being searched, and because the driver had no licence and no insurance, his car would be impounded.

When the policewoman finished searching my bag, she turned around for two seconds to see what was happening to the others, because there was such commotion. I quickly dumped my gear from my waistband into my handbag. I was then put into the back of the police car because they wanted to take me to the station for a strip search. It is so degrading, with people looking at you as you stand there with the police. I carried on chatting to the police officer about the fact that I was off drugs because I had an implant. It wasn't a complete lie. I only had two slip-ups in four months, which isn't bad going for me. At the station I had my strip search and the policewoman fortunately ignored my handbag because she had already searched it. I had survived by the skin of my teeth, but it really made me think hard about what I was doing.

I had to get Lee to come and collect me, and I could see in his face that he knew that I had been up to something. I just told him that I had been out with Paul and his friend. I felt so stupid and so guilty, but I didn't want to own up to what I had been doing. I think Lee was just glad to see that I was safe, so we returned back to his house. I tried to wait as long as possible before sneaking into the toilet to have a couple of lines of gear. I must have been on a different planet to think that Lee wouldn't hear the tin foil rustling. Looking back on this incident makes me realise that I had been very selfish. I don't know whether I did it because I could, or because I thought to myself that Lee had smoked gear around me when I was clean so I could do the same to him. It was not a nice thing to do to somebody who hadn't been off the gear for very long.

I am not a violent person by nature, but something snapped inside me when Lee questioned whether I had just been using in the toilet. I lost the plot, as they say. He didn't shout or ask me in a nasty manner, because he wasn't like that. I walked into the bedroom, pushed the door shut, and begun to punch it. Perhaps I was angry with myself for being so stupid, or angry that I had been caught out. Whatever the reason, the anger seemed to come from nowhere. Normally, Lee and I never argued, because he was far too laid back. Normally, I wasn't one to shout and get mad either. The anger just surfaced for a second and then it was over. I didn't realise until a few minutes afterwards, that I had damaged my hand badly. I came out of the bedroom, and by this time Lee had wandered off to let me cool down. I shouted to Lee to come and look at what I had done to myself. I think at first that he thought that I was exaggerating, but when he saw how bad it was, he soon changed his mind. I couldn't feel the pain when I was hitting the door, because I had just had some gear. It was the first and last time that I lost control. After this incident I kept away from people who were still using.

AMSTERDAM

Lee and I made plans for a trip to Amsterdam because this was something that Lee wanted to do with me for sometime. We only planned to go for a few days and we thought it would be an opportunity to get away from our little town. I wasn't feeling as good as I had wanted to, which was my fault as I had used for a couple of days before, and the heroin still had to come out of my system. This was one occasion when a trip abroad didn't hold the usual excitement for me. We drove to the car ferry port at Harwich. It had been years since I had been on a ferry, so I began to look forward to the journey and the short break in Amsterdam. We made ourselves comfortable on a seat near a window. I've always been the same since a child, whenever we went away, on a plane or any other journey, I always liked to be able to look out of the window, and watch the world go by. The restaurant on board looked very posh and we asked the waiter if we could have a table. It was a set price menu, where you could eat what you wanted. Everything was set out so beautifully on tables, and the food was delicious. We decided to make use of the cinema on the way home, but this time we wanted to explore the boat and just relax. After we disembarked at the Hook of Holland, we had to get onto a train to Amsterdam.

We hadn't booked a hotel in advance so we had to tramp the streets with our suitcases to find one. The first hotel looked more like a hostel to me, but we booked in and put are things in the room. The room was very small and it didn't feel right from the second I set foot in it. I was prepared to put up with it for a couple of days, when I glanced out of the window and saw an elderly man who was smoking heroin. He was in a little alley just below where we were staying. He paced up and down unsteadily as if intoxicated. That was enough for me. I wanted to get out of that place immediately. I didn't like it from the beginning and that just finished making up my mind. I couldn't believe it: wherever I went, heroin was there to haunt me. We had come all this way to get away from the reminders of heroin, and there it was again, right in our faces.

We checked out and started walking along the cobbled streets until we came to another hotel that looked much better. It was much more suitable, and I felt a lot safer there. That evening I felt as though I just wanted to curl up and fall asleep, but Lee wanted to make the most of our stay in Amsterdam. We wrapped ourselves up because it was a lot colder than when we had left home. I felt the cold weather badly because I had been using only a couple of days previously so I was more sensitive. This wasn't what I expected Amsterdam to look like. We went to a little bar to have a drink, attracted by the green neon lights that made it stand out against the other bars. We then decided to explore some more so that I could see what Amsterdam really looked like. I was mesmerised by the canals and shop after shop. There was such an old feel to the city. Lee had spent time there years ago when he and a group of lads went on a mad weekend, and by what they told me it sounded like a really crazy place. We walked past the red-light district, and I could see all these attractive looking girls standing in the windows. Some of them looked like models, and I couldn't believe that these women thought that this was the only way of earning money. Legalised prostitution may be acceptable in some countries, but cannot see it being acceptable in Britain. I can see the arguments in favour of legalising this profession, but I am not completely convinced that it would be a good thing at home. It struck me as quite bizarre.

We woke up around ten in the morning and went to have breakfast. Afterwards we walked by all the little coffee shops and decided to go in one to have a look at what it was like. As we walked in we were met by an overwhelming odour of cannabis. Personally I have always liked the smell. It seemed that everywhere you went you could smell the distinctive smell. We ordered ourselves a drink and looked at the menu we were given. The only things on the menu were various types of cannabis. There were names like Bubblegum, Purplehaze, Northernlights, Whitewidow, Greenspecial, and Silver shadow. These were all different kinds of marijuana plants (skunk). They also had ready rolled joints to smoke, and at the counter there were big fridges, like you have in a bakery, full of skunk. Normally I don't smoke pot because I always feel so paranoid on the stuff, but at the time in Amsterdam we thought we would do what the natives do.

We bought several different kinds and sat there on a different planet. Everything came across so funny. I was also very hungry and felt I could eat for England and probably Holland too. We went into so many different coffee shops that I lost count. At every few steps we were approached guys wanting to sell us ecstasy pills. We decided to purchase a few but we got ripped off because the pills turned out to be Smints (sweets). After this lesson in duplicity we were more careful. We ended up with some blue pills with a shotgun logo on them. We had half of one tablet each, as Lee remembered from his previous visit that they were very strong. Nothing like the poor quality pills that you get in England. Lee told me that they were different in a lot of ways, because they made you feel on a high for much longer, and they didn't prevent you sleeping, unlike the English pills. The Dutch pills also let you wake up the next day feeling as fresh as a daisy, and feeling hungry. I had bad experience on English pills, because they stop you sleeping and you feel rough for days afterwards. We also went into a mushroom shop that obviously didn't sell your normal everyday mushrooms. It was full of things like natural pills that give you a high, special 'come down' kits for the Monday after, and pill testing kits. We decided on buying one of these kits, because we had been ripped off once already.

The way the testing kit worked was to break off a small bit of a pill on to a plate or something that was acid resistant. Then you put a drop of the tester liquid onto the pill. If it turned black it meant it was ecstasy, if it turned yellow it indicated amphetamines. This little kit was useful if you wanted to make your night a little safer, but to be perfectly honest, if you want to have a good night out don't take anything. It is much safer and at least you will hang onto your brain cells. Pills and other social drugs are noted for destroying brain cells. Our little trip to Amsterdam was very enjoyable, but could have been a whole lot better if I had not been thinking about the gear again.

Lee loves to DJ (mixing records) and I would often sit in his room listening to him practice the art of 'mixing' music. He was such a perfectionist that if he messed up a mix, he would start all over again, even if he had recorded an hour's work on tape or CD. Lee has a good ear for music, and is very creative and versatile. He played the violin up to grade eight standard. If he had finished the last grade he could have become a violin teacher. When he was sixteen years old, one of his best friends committed suicide by hanging himself, and the trauma had a significant effect on Lee. This may have contributed to the reason why Lee never finished his violin exams, but using drugs would not have helped either.

We had periods off and on the gear, but other than that we really tried to live our lives as normal as possible. We would eat out a lot and do lots of swimming, go to the cinema. I wanted to get my self a little part time job to keep myself busy and I needed the cash. I was scanning through when the perfect one came up in the local newspaper. A small stables was advertising for a stable hand, back in my hometown. I had done an awful lot of work at riding stables before, and I also knew a lot of local people associated with horses. The stable owner remembered me from when I had given lessons to her daughters all those years ago. So I got Lee to drop me at the stable yard so I could meet my new boss, and also have a look around to see what work needed doing. It was great to be back in stables again, and the owner was confident that I would soon get to grips with the role. There was about an acre of land, four stables that didn't look particularly safe, a shed that had all the riding equipment in, and a barn where all the hay and straw was kept. I was back in my element again. I was in my comfort zone, with animals and the outdoors.

There were two ponies called Blue and Sonny, a Shetland pony called Teddy, who actually looked like a cute little teddy bear. There was also a sheep called Lambrusco, and two goats; Chianti and Chablis. We gave them all nicknames, which I felt were much more appropriate. Lambrusco was called Lucy, Chablis was named Smiler because she always looked so happy to see us, and Chianti was nicknamed Three-legs because she had suffered a stroke and only had the use of three of her legs. My mornings were occupied mucking out, feeding, and exercising the ponies. Sometimes I got Lee out jogging with them. Lee and the ponies both got exercise, which they needed, and I thought it was really nice of him to take part in doing this work for me. The part I loved most of all was riding again. I found it very therapeutic. In the summer I would go down to the bottom of the field and knock off the plums and apples that were out of reach of the animals before they dropped off. I thought of them as mine. In a way I thought of myself as my own boss, because I virtually had the stables to myself all day.

Lee and I continued to struggle with getting ourselves entirely off of the gear. The major problem was money: we just could not afford our heroin habits. We then did something that I regret to this day. We started selling heroin: we became dealers. We just sold enough so that we could pay for our habits. We were certainly not doing it for the money, and we knew that what we were doing was totally wrong, but addiction to heroin clouds your moral judgement and can make you do anything.

The following anecdotes illustrate just how dangerous the life of a heroin addict can be. There is nothing special or usual in these episodes that makes them any different to the sort of things that most addicts contend with on a day-to-day basis. Danger and risk are daily companions for the addict: the danger of being robbed or beaten, and the risk of being apprehended by officers of the law. Under this pressure it is not surprising that addicts become secretive and paranoid about where they get their drugs from, where they keep them, and where they use them. Likewise, dealers or sellers of drugs are just as paranoid about whom they sell to and where they can be contacted. Experience has taught both sellers and buyers to be circumspect and to construct complicated strategies to avoid detection. Robbery and violence are commonplace between those who inhabit this secretive world, even if it rarely spills over into the real world.

One day we had been to get our gear, and we had an acquaintance with us who introduced us to a group of young lads. We sold gear to them a few times after that, and there were no trouble. However, one evening I had a phone call from one of them asking if we could get some gear for them. We had just been to collect our gear again, and on this occasion we had Paul and his new girlfriend with him. By this time Paul and I had put everything behind us. I wanted to stay friends with him because we had so much history together.

We had put the rest of our gear away and just had the gear for the guy who had phoned. When we pulled up at the place we arranged to meet, I begun to feel uneasy and worried. I thought it was all a little strange that he had asked us to meet in a park where there weren't many people around. We were parked facing a hedge, and then I heard a car approach. It turned out to be a big green vehicle that pulled in behind us, trapping us so we couldn't reverse out. Six young men jumped out of the vehicle and came over to us, so Lee wound down his window slightly to give them the stuff. At this point their attitude changed and they pulled out knives and screwdrivers shouting to us to hand over the gear. One of them punched Lee through the window to intimidate us into handing over all our gear. By this time I was in shock, and I dropped the gear on the floor in panic. Fortunately, Lee had his seat belt on and all the doors were locked, because they tried to pull him out of the car but couldn't manage to unlock his door through the gap in the window. I was trying to find the gear, because I thought that the best thing to do was give them what they wanted and then they would leave us alone. I was convinced that if we didn't hand over the stuff then we were going to get stabbed.

Meanwhile, Lee was getting punched over and over again. I was also punched in the back of the head, but didn't really feel it, as I was in such a shocked state. There were hands coming in through the window from all directions, still punching and trying to strangle Lee. One of the gang snapped the key off in the ignition to prevent us escaping. This made the situation a hundred times worse, because we were completely trapped and unable to escape. I eventually found the gear, which I threw at one of the gang just to get them to leave. One of them even grabbed my handbag, and because I had everything in it; my cards, keys and some small change, I ran after the man and forced him to throw it back to me. Lee's wallet was also stolen during the fight. He didn't even notice until later. Fortunately the gang couldn't get to the back seats because Paul and his girlfriend had a lot of money, which the gang didn't know about.

We all sat there in shock after they drove away. After a while we found the other half of the key on the floor. By a stroke of luck, Lee was able to push it into the other half stuck in the ignition so that we could start the car. We were so scared that we just wanted to get back to Paul's home to sit down and have a smoke to calm our nerves. It was a terrifying experience. The following day, the persistent fear and shock actually prevented me from leaving the safety of the house, and I kept bursting into tears.

Even when you are dealing, you are not immune from being ripped off and beaten up. As a small dealer you are just one step up the ladder from an ordinary user, and hence you are always vulnerable. You still have to buy gear from a bigger dealer further up the ladder.

The more gear you buy the more the risk of being robbed, and the greater the penalty if the police pick you up. Sometimes it was so difficult to get gear from our usual contacts, that we had to ask other people to score for us from their contacts. We would have to put our trust in somebody else. Heroin addicts and dealers are not exactly the most trustworthy people on Earth. There was always the risk that they might run off with our money, or the gear they got us would turn out to be face powder or something similar. Even if it is genuine gear, there is no guarantee about the quality. Heroin that is sold at street level is never pure; it is cut (diluted) with other substances such as brick dust or paracetamol. Sometimes it is cut so much that there is barely any heroin left, but to test for the quantity of heroin is way beyond the technical competence of the average user. As a result the user has to put up with whatever they can get.

One day we asked one of the guys who lived in the next village to score some gear for us, which involved travelling further than usual to get it. Alan, who was getting it for us, then had to go through somebody else because he didn't know the dealer himself. We had gone through the process with this other person a few times before without any problems, so this time we asked him directly to get it for us, to save having to go through Alan as well. It may sound hugely complicated, but this is normal, and all part of the life style of a drug addict.

His nickname was Soggy and it really suited him. He looked wet and pathetic just like his nickname, and he was as thick as two short planks. We made a deal with him that we would give him some gear in return for getting our supply for us. We picked him up because he lived on the way to where he was going to get our gear. On this occasion I was a little concerned, because he kept receiving phone calls on the journey and whispering. He explained it away by saying that he needed to get some gear for the people on the phone, after getting some for us. Lee and I had run out of gear early that morning, so we were beginning to feel the worse for wear, and just wanted to get the deal over and done with as soon as possible. Soggy said to somebody on the phone how far away he was from where we needed to go, and it was only afterwards that we realised this was because they had arranged to pick him up. We arrived at the usual place and it was starting to get dark by this stage. I told Lee to stick with Soggy, and not to leave his side, as they both walked off down the street to meet the dealer. I just had a feeling that his body language was different on this occasion and there was something wrong. They were meeting the dealer in exactly the same spot as usual, but Soggy darted off in front of Lee.

I had sat in the car for at least ten minutes when Lee arrived back on his own. Soggy had left Lee at the end of the road; while he walked up the side street where he always met the dealer. It was just a minute later that Lee looked up the side street only to find that Soggy had disappeared. Soggy had run off through an adjoining street after scoring with the dealer. He had stolen our gear, and Lee's mobile phone as well. We barely had enough money for the petrol for the journey back home.

We went to a phone box to ring Lee's mobile, but obviously there was no answer. We also went back to the place where Soggy had scored from to see if we could see him but there was no sign of him anywhere. Lee had spotted the dealer before from a distance so he had an idea what he looked like. As luck would have it, we spotted the dealer hanging about to meet someone else, so we went up to him to ask if he had seen Soggy. We explained that Soggy had taken our money and not returned with our gear. He looked at us suspiciously in case we were police. Dealers are notoriously paranoid about strangers, with good reason. The dealer told us that Soggy had walked in the opposite direction to where our car was parked. He advised us to keep looking for Soggy.

Twenty minutes later, after searching the streets for Soggy, we bumped into the dealer for a second time. By this time I was nearly in tears and he could see I wasn't lying. I told him that the money Soggy had been bringing him every day was ours, and that it would be much easier if we dealt with him directly. I had nothing to lose by asking the dealer to lend us some gear. I offered to leave something valuable as security until the next day. Lee had an expensive violin in the boot of his car that had a mother of pearl bow, but he wasn't really interested in what we offered as security. There aren't many dealers that would have trusted our word and helped us out like he did. In fact dealers like this are as plentiful as rocking-horse manure.

The dealer wanted to know for certain that we were genuine heroin addicts. The problem was that neither Lee nor I looked like addicts: we were too well dressed and too presentable. The dealer got into our car and watched our every move. He needed to double-check everything for his own sake, because we could have been police for all he knew. Eventually he passed us some gear and watched us put a tiny bit on some tin foil, and watched us smoke it, just to check we were telling the truth. The skill and speed that Lee prepared the tube and smoked the heroin convinced the dealer that we were genuine users. By this time we had been withdrawing for hours and were desperate for heroin.

Lee and I really tried our hardest to keep ourselves off heroin. We tried many different ways again and again. We didn't loose hope and faith, and that was a real positive attitude to carry while going through all of the up's and down's we were having. There was only one occasion Lee and I had a little fall out, and didn't see each other much for a bit. Other than that our friendship has been like a rock, and that is something I will always cherish. We have always stayed to true to one another, even if it was another gear relationship.

I was still working at the stables, but something terrible happened which upset Lee and me for a long time afterwards. One of the local addicts decided to occupy the little tack-room and to sleep rough up there in the loft. I had heard that he was even inviting people up there for barbecues, although I never saw it happen. There is hay and straw everywhere, and he could have set the whole place alight. He should not have been there anyway because it was private property. My boss went up there one particular Sunday and she caught him in there. His excuse to her was that I had allowed him to stay there, so my boss called me to get to the bottom of things. I had a slight hangover that morning so it is possible that I didn't sound too convincing when I denied his allegation. I couldn't believe that she would accept his word above mine, but she did, and she asked me to collect my things and hand in the keys. I tried reasoning with her, but it was no good. Yet again I had something that I loved taken from me. If I had known that he had been up there I would called the police or even escorted him off the premises myself, but I was the last to find out any of this.

I was devastated, because I had grown so attached to the animals. This episode really knocked me back. I felt as if my life was washed up and nothing seemed to go right for me. Once again I was jobless, and feeling low and upset.

Lee and I had patches on and off the gear and this time that we had fallen back into the heroin trap, so we decided to go away to Tenerife. I had been living with Lee for just over a year by this stage, and we had been together for nearly two years. We planned to do a detox in the same way as I had done in Cyprus, but this time I took some sleeping tablets with me, and a couple of morphine capsules, that had been prescribed by the clinic in London quite some time before. I had never taken morphine before so I wasn't sure how I would react to them. The first night I took one, it made me violently sick, and the heat made it even worse. After that we didn't bother with anything apart from the sleeping tablets, which we needed to help us get some rest over the next twelve days we spent there.

This was another extremely difficult detox for us. The first few days were the hardest during our stay in Tenerife, but after that we started to get out in the sun to do some swimming and a bit of walking. You feel as though you've aged sixty years when you first coming off heroin. In my experience, each time I do a detox it is unlike any other. Sometimes it is very hard and at other times a bit easier. I think even when I was at my lowest, because I was so young, I found it extremely hard to get myself back to normal again. I suppose being on heroin was my comfort zone. For me it was normal because I had been on the drug for so long. Perhaps that is why I kept having relapses and why my illness kept going on and on. Doing a detox is hard enough, but staying off heroin is even harder. Most users will tell you the same thing.

We had a great time near the end of our time away. We even went on a trip to a zoo. There was also a swimming pool, loads of animals and a dolphin show. We watched the dolphin show because I just love dolphins. I think they are amazing and I sat mesmerised by them. The aquatic instructors got in the pool with the dolphins as they performed different tricks. The accompanying music was just perfect for what they were doing. I was overwhelmed by the whole spectacle. I had never seen anything quite like it. I was reduced to tears by my emotions and didn't want anyone to notice. Anyone who tries stopping heroin without any form of medication has an overwhelming awareness of their feelings and this definitely reduces you to tears. I took deep breaths to try to hold back the tears of joy, but there was no stopping it.

We had some lovely meals while we were away and made the most of the rest of are time in the sun. The only problem was I had eaten something that upset my stomach the day before, so when we came home I was again back in my bed and not feeling at all well.

I've done some lovely things in my life even though this drug has been there from my early teens. I have been lucky to have the support of my friends and family, because I know there are a lot of people who have no support at all. How they survive without support is a mystery to me.

A REAL FRIEND

One of the legitimate ways that I discovered for earning money was to tour the neighbourhood asking people if I could clean their cars. I had a bucket and a knapsack full of cleaning materials so I actually looked quite professional. I felt slightly embarrassed that I was doing car washing at my age, but I also felt it was better than stealing or getting into some kind of trouble. I felt good when I looked at my finished handiwork. At least I was not out burgling houses or taking money from people in the street. I was proud to be doing something honest.

One particular customer called Brian was a very kind man who gave me a bucket of hot water to clean his car because it was a very cold day. Afterwards, he made me a turkey sandwich because he said I looked as if I needed a square meal because I was so skinny. He also gave me some hand cream to rub into my hands because they were red and chapped, and he warned me to look after such pretty hands. Finally he gave me a banana and a chocolate bar to take with me. He was one of the few people in the town that treated me with kindness and respect. I later found out that at the time he had no idea who I was or anything about my history.

About two weeks later, when I was short of money and desperate to score, I paid Brian another visit in the hope that he would want his car washing again. Most of my other customers had refused because the weather was so bad and I thought he would refuse too, so in desperation I started out by asking if he would lend me some money. I even offered to leave my Income Support Book, which is what social benefits were paid into at the time. Amazingly he said that he trusted me and would give me some money in advance, and that I could come back the following week to clean his car. He mentioned that I looked anorexic and offered me some food. Once again he only showed me respect, kindness and generosity. Much later, he admitted that his neighbours had told him who I was, but he never made any reference to this, nor was he judgemental in any way. He was not like anybody I had ever met before. He is still my friend to this day and has been the best friend I could ever have asked for. I didn't recognise it at the time, but he was the guardian angel I had always been looking for.

Lee and I had a final time away together and we went to Butlins. Our relationship had been on and off for quite a period of time now. I felt that this was it: we needed to get our acts together. I really wanted to make a go of stopping for good. Enough was enough. I wanted to make a life for myself because I'd missed so much. Whatever it took I was going to try and make a change. We were planning on doing a detox and then get ourselves onto Naltrexone tablets. This is an oral version of the implants I had used so far. Implants are extremely expensive and beyond the resources of most addicts. My family had reached the point where they could no longer fund these private treatments. I felt that Lee had something on his mind, but I was just too unwell to worry about it at the time.

When we returned from Butlins I went back to my Mums. Lee decided to go round to Paul's place so he could keep himself busy. I really thought that I would be meeting up with them later that day, but when I tried to telephone Lee later that day, he didn't answer. I felt so lonely; I just wanted someone to sit with who was experiencing the same thing as me. I didn't know, until he told me later, that Lee had made the decision that we needed to stay away from one another, if we wanted the detox to work. Instead, I was left in the dark wondering why I was being ignored. If he had of spoken to me, I think I would have been able to come to terms with it. I felt terrible: my mind was all over the place. I needed some friends for company to cheer me up, but all my friends who were non-users were also friends of Lee. I didn't know whom to turn to. I was so depressed, and I desperately wanted to make a success of staying off the gear.

My Mum was so concerned she took me to the doctors, because I couldn't stop crying. Everything was suddenly hitting home. I had made a complete mess of my life during all those years of drug abuse. I had hurt so many people. It was even painful just thinking about it. All I ever wanted was to be normal, just like everybody else, to be happy, and to make something of my life. I was submerged in self-pity and remorse. For a time I thought I might be losing my mind, or perhaps there was something else wrong with me.

My appointment with my doctor did little to help. I was given some tablets and told to get some counselling. Mum tried to explain that I had a problem with heroin since an early age, but he wasn't my usual doctor, and didn't seem interested in my problems. I was so depressed that I even considered taking my own life. When I got back home I began taking the antidepressants that the doctor had prescribed. They didn't start to work until about a week later, and in my usual impatient way I didn't even give them a chance. In my true Marie style I began to tell myself that heroin was going to be my life, so what was the point in denying it? I felt the same as I did when I was fifteen, sitting at home with nobody to go out with or even talk to, and I did what I did at that age: I went out and used. The only people that I could go and sit with were addicts like me. I know that you will think that I was stupid to resort to heroin again, and the only defence I have is that I was so depressed. Perhaps this was the reason I always went back to heroin.

I was angry for quite a few months; about the way that Lee had left me. I couldn't understand his reasons for leaving, because it couldn't have been about our relationship. Heroin addicts don't really have relationships. What concerned me most was that I thought we were friends, and friends don't treat one another that way. Obviously he had changed, and I didn't like the person he had changed into. I had lost a very good friend. I know that I let myself down when I started using again, and when I bumped into Lee later, I could tell that he was using too. Perhaps if we had remained friends we could have supported each other. He had hurt me and I was still angry enough to want revenge. I told Lee that I was pregnant, just to see his reaction. He didn't know what to say. I know that it was cruel to play such a trick on him, but revenge doesn't care about cruelty. Revenge is all about inflicting pain and suffering, but in this case it didn't work out that way.

I had put my Mum through too much stress and she needed a break. My addiction to heroin had started its work on splitting my family and me apart. I had a choice, but I was too mixed up and depressed to even contemplate getting clean at that point. Previously my mum and dad had been there to give me that little push towards getting off it. Looking back at the early days, I suppose I wasn't entirely ready at times to get off heroin. It is such a deep-rooted addiction that you need to be totally committed and to really want to give it up, before you have a chance of being successful. I had been a rebellious, immature kid for all those years and I now I was a twenty-three year old woman with the same problems. My addiction had robbed me of nine years of my life, and I was still not equipped to lead a normal life.

I started to live at one of the doss houses in my hometown where drug users congregate. The couple that rented the place were good enough to rent me a room, but there were times when I was very unhappy there. It was difficult living at this house, because things would go missing, like food and clothes. I have lost count of the times I have had clothes stolen from me while I have been staying at different places. I have also had people doing spiteful things, like cutting up my clothes. I don't think I ever did anything to deserve this sort of treatment. I cleaned and cooked for the people I lived with. Kath, my landlord, was on dialysis for her kidneys, so she was extremely ill. Her husband had varicose veins from injecting heroin, so he and was in a bad way too. The house didn't really get cleaned unless I did it.

I started speaking to Lee again as he had gone back on the gear again and we begun to get close again, but just as friends. He apologised and told me he was influenced by other people telling him to stay away from me. I just wished he hadn't listened, because I was very hurt at the time. We both agreed that this arrangement was the best for both of us, because our experience told us that two addicts together just doesn't work. It didn't work with Mick, or Paul or Lee. You need to get it together by yourself, but as long as you have support and people there to speak to, it definitely helps a lot.

There were so many rumours going around the town about me, and I know that small-minded jealous people spread them. There were rumours saying that I was selling myself for half a bag of heroin a time, which wasn't true at all. If you can think of anything nasty then you can bet that I was called it. It was very hurtful at the time, but now that I am older I just ignore the insults and let it go. Mostly it was a case of the pot calling the kettle black. A lot of people, who labelled me a 'smack head', take Class A drugs themselves, like pills or coke.

I often find that people are very nosey. What I do with my life is my business. I don't poke my nose into other people's affairs, so why should they do it to me. Perhaps it is because people know that I am a heroin addict, and they are curious to know more. I find it intensely irritating. Sometimes I walk into shops and I am spoken to quite rudely. Maybe it is because I have a bad reputation, but that no excuse for rudeness. I have certainly never been rude to them.

My experience of living in a doss house full of users wasn't great. I remember feeling totally alone at one stage, because I had fallen out with the people I was living with. It was something so trivial and even though there were some really horrible times, there were also some nice moments when they treated me like their daughter. I walked around the streets not knowing where to go. I felt alone and so depressed that my life had reach such a dismal state. I looked with envy at all the happy young people walking past, hand in hand, laughing and enjoying themselves. I wondered what I would be doing now if I hadn't touched heroin. One thing is for certain; I knew I wouldn't be walking around the streets late at night alone with nowhere to go. I would probably be in my own home, in the warm with people who loved me and trusted me and who I trusted. I knew that everyone in my family still loved me, but I had all too often abused their trust. I just wished we could be a close family again. Instead I had lost the trust of those who loved me, and I only trusted myself and nobody else. I was also extremely paranoid about anything anyone said to me. Heroin was changing my personality, just like it changed everybody else's. One way or another, heroin was making my world a very lonely place.

I sat around for some time in the cold wondering if I should go and knock on an old friend's door. She wasn't on heroin, but she did take other drugs occasionally. When I finally got to her little house I tapped on the door, because I didn't want wake up her one-year son. I told her that I needed somewhere to stay just for a couple of days. She agreed as long as I didn't smoke gear in the house. I kept telling her I would never do that, besides I hadn't got any gear anyway, although I wished I had. I don't think she was listening, because she said it again later, just before I went to sleep on the couch. It was very good of her to let me stay. I didn't even want to say anything about how depressed I felt or that I was going through a rough patch. All I wanted to do was fall asleep and try to forget everything. I was woken up by footsteps passing through the living room to the kitchen. It was my friend and her ex-boyfriend taking crack cocaine. What she did was her business, but it struck me as hypocritical for her to be so concerned about me smoking heroin in the house when she was doing crack. On the other hand, I suppose she had the right to lay down the law in her own house. A lot of people don't realise that it is the same as smoking cigarettes, whoever is in the house inhales the smoke, whether it is tobacco, or heroin or crack.

I had a friend who I stayed with on a separate occasion, who had a young boy and another child on the way. She didn't want another child, because she said it had been an accident and she was no longer in touch with the father. It was quite sad and sickening to see her taking whatever she could get her hands on to try and kill the baby. She took heroin, crack, inhaled gas, swallowed countless tablets, drank excessively and did who knows what else to harm herself and her unborn child. I was there the day she went into labour, and I took her to hospital. The next day I went to the hospital with Lee to see how they both were. I am crying now as I write this, because I remember seeing her baby in so much pain. The screams were unlike any baby screams I had ever heard before. The little infant was twitching and shaking from the crack, and sneezing from the heroin withdrawal symptoms. That poor baby was in intensive care for weeks, with only the nurses to care for it. I know that when she finally got the baby back it wasn't right. It didn't make eye contact like other babies. It was so sad seeing it like that. Fortunately I only stayed with that girl for a couple of days.

After a few days I went back to live at the dos house again. Lee and I also started to sell heroin again as I just couldn't pay for my habit. I only sold to a very limited number of people who I had known for years. So Lee and I would see each other once a day to sort out money and gear so that we could both get by.

I had put in an application for a flat on the housing list. Technically I was classified as homeless so I was reasonably high on the list. Nevertheless it would a waiting game, and I was never very good at that. I was in a difficult situation having to keep moving around all the time. I had already over-stayed my welcome at home. The stress had been too much for them. I had to sort my problems out on my own.

There was actually a time when I was living at this particular house, that I sat and did a detox while other people were doing heroin around me. It was at a time when I wasn't selling heroin and I was struggling to get any money, because even car washing wasn't profitable enough. Anyway it had been about a week where I had been using such a tiny amount, and I was withdrawing more often than not. To make matters worse, the couple I was living with at the dos house threatened to evict me if I didn't get clean, even though they were still using. I never knew why they did this. Maybe it was because they cared and wanted to see me clean, or maybe it was because they wanted to control me, who knows. I didn't want to be homeless yet again so I had to resort to desperate measures. I had a few Subutex tablets (a medication used as a heroin substitute) that somebody had given me but I was always scared of taking these, because they had made me quite poorly, on an earlier occasion. It had been around 17 hours since I had used anything and I was 'roasting' (withdrawing). Regardless of my fears, I was put in a position where I had no choice other than to take a small piece of a tablet. I sat there panicking that it was going to make me ill. Half an hour went by and surprisingly I felt slightly better. It was the first time that Subutex had ever done that to me.

I sat watching TV trying to keep my mind off of gear, when a guy called Barry came around, sat down and started smoking gear. I just froze, because I couldn't believe that nobody said anything. Chris and Katie brought some off him. I couldn't believe that they were doing that to me when they had just virtually forced me to start my detox. I felt like they were doing it on purpose, to be cruel and this was something I would never forget.

There were countless times when I broke the law and never got caught. I remember one instance vividly. At one time I stayed with a lady who had been extremely kind to me. Sasha wanted to help me stop the gear, because she told me I was worth saving. While I was staying there I took some baby clothes and a necklace that was of very great sentimental value to her. Her father had bought it for her before he passed away. She had about thirty different necklaces, rings and different pieces of gold jewellery in a box, and I only took the one to sell. I sincerely regret that I did such a thing to her, because she was trying so hard to help me. I have never forgiven myself, and I regret to this day that I acted in such a way.

Sasha eventually found me and beat me up, and I ended up in hospital because she hit me so many times my head was swollen. She also hit me again while I was on one of my car washing jobs. I know I did wrong, but I think her reaction was a bit extreme. Whichever way you look at it, she had assaulted me, but I suppose she had been severely provoked.

I stayed with my older sister, Karla, for a short time when she returned from Birmingham. I stayed with my sister because she needed help with her young son Cameron. Karla knew that I was struggling with the gear, because I was completely honest with her about it. I don't think she could grasp that I couldn't just stop it without medication with a simple click of the fingers.

Karla asked me to go to the cash point one day for her and also to the shop to get her a few things, so she gave me her pin number and off I went. Some days later, when I had no money I noticed her card was on the table. I had been withdrawing for hours and wasn't thinking straight, so I gave way to temptation and took the card. Karla had ordered herself a new card, so she had two, and would often leave the old one laying about. This was too easy for me, so I thought I would just take a bit here and there. I remember every time I went to draw some money out I had a strange mixture of guilt and an adrenalin rush. I took a little cash out every day for about a month. When my sister found out she had me arrested and I was put on probation. Obviously she did the right thing. She knows that I love her, and that my heroin addiction had yet again got the better of me. I hate writing this, and you would have thought I would have learnt from what had happened with my eldest sister, Lucy, some years earlier. My older sister and I are very close now and we have put this episode behind us.

One day Lee and I couldn't get any gear, so we made a trip over to Rushdean to see Tody, the guy who had an accident with a car running him down. He was selling heroin at the time, so he was the next in line to call for our heroin. We knocked on his door and it seemed ages before he answered it. I looked around his small, smelly flat that didn't really have much in it apart from a couple of old chairs and a tiny TV for him to watch. To be honest, there aren't many users on heroin that have nice, clean flats; they are mostly messy and devoid of furniture.

We sat smoking our gear when Tody said he had been having a lot of trouble with some blokes who lived in Rushdean. The small window in his front door had been smashed, and he told us that they had also come in with a hammer and made him hand over all his gear. He also said that he had trouble with getting in his gear (injecting), because he had bad abscesses all over his body. It wasn't until he rolled up his trousers that I realised how bad they really were. There were huge lumps on his legs with puss coming out; I had never seen anything quite like it.

We had to go again the following day and as we walked in there was a really strong smell that reminded me of rotting flesh. Tody had been injecting into holes and abscesses, but that's how it gets some people. You are so desperate to get the gear into your system that you will go through pain and agony to make you feel better at the end of it. I felt a little sorry for him, but I also felt he was slightly mad because he can't have any self-respect. What he really needed was strong antibiotics to help clear the infection and to stop injecting all together. I found out a week later that he had been taken into hospital because he was close to losing his legs.

A HOME OF MY OWN

You might say that all my troubles are self-inflicted and that I only have myself to blame. I can't argue with that, but in my defence you have to remember that I was so young and ignorant when I first became addicted to heroin. Unlike other drugs, it is both physically and mentally addictive. Addiction is an illness with no simple cure. If you are ill and in severe pain, what do you do? You reach out for some medication that you know will cure the pain. This is exactly what addicts do. Heroin addicts need their gear just like diabetics need their insulin. Addicts do desperate and despicable things simply to get their medication. Even after a detox, the addiction remains with you, and whenever you have painful or unpleasant experiences you reach out for the familiar medication. This is the reason why most addicts including me slip up so often.

Few people know that after the American civil war, huge numbers of soldiers returned from the battlefields with horrific war wounds, for which the only treatment was morphine, to relieve the pain. Those that didn't die of their wounds became morphine addicts: hundreds of thousands of them. Fortunately at that time, morphine was freely available and legal. It wasn't until some 70 years later that these drugs were classified and restricted. Even around the turn of the 20th century, heroin kits could be purchased by mail order. If this were still the case, then my life would have been so different. Dealers, doss houses, and my whole life style would not even exist. I am not advocating that we should legalise drugs, I just want people to recognise that addiction is an illness and that treatment for it should be more openly available without the stigma.

I've always wanted to help others and maybe one day I will have the opportunity to do so. I have always wanted to go into schools and share my story with children. I think children respond much better if there is a real living example in front of them. The drugs education that I had was just a few leaflets handed around that seemed irrelevant to me, and which I didn't take seriously.

I had arranged for my mail to be redirected to Lee's house, because I didn't trust anybody where I had been staying previously. I applied for a flat of my own because I was officially classed as homeless and therefore a high priority case. It wasn't long before Lee called to tell me I had some mail, so I told him to open it. I had been offered a flat and I think Lee was as excited and overjoyed as I was. He knew how much I needed my own place. I could finally get out of the house I'd been living in.

I had been selling and doing a lot more gear than usual, and I was also getting myself a 'crack' habit (cocaine). At the time I really couldn't see how terrible I looked, but I know now after seeing pictures of myself, that I didn't look like me one bit. My looks had completely gone altogether, and I was thinner than when I lived with Paul in Rushdean. Crack was what really did it for me and made a huge impact in my life in many ways. The couple I was living with had a 'crack' habit, so it was always around me. This was quite a new thing for me, but I found myself getting more and more into it. I hated it, because it made me feel paranoid, anti-social, and I wouldn't want to speak to anybody. It's an extremely strange drug and very addictive, but only mentally addictive. There is virtually no physical dependence. I've seen people get themselves in a huge mess when taking it.

By now I was doing crack everyday, and going further and further down hill. I had to travel everyday to buy my heroin and crack, and this meant getting a lift from someone with a car. I'd usually give whoever gave me a lift some heroin or crack as payment. Paul usually took us to get our gear and crack and then we would go and smoke it somewhere. Most people cant wait to open it up and smoke it the second they get it. Some even kept their crack pipe with them, but I didn't.

Three weeks went by before I eventually got the keys to my new flat. When I arrived and opened the door I had a huge sense of joy and relief knowing I was going to be able to do as I please, when I please, and all my things were going to be safe. I looked around the flat and noticed it really needed some attention because an elderly couple had lived there previous to me. The kitchen was the only room that had been re-decorated by the housing association. The rest of the place was really bad and it had a funny, musty smell to the place.

My dad, his girlfriend and my mum were there most weekends doing all they could to help make it homely for me. This was a great help because I wouldn't have been able to do it alone. My mum spent a lot of time there when I wasn't around to surprise me, like putting up pictures and curtains. The rest of the furniture was given to me and I used throw-overs and big cushions to make it look more modern. I was so happy. My dad also bought me a new washing machine, cooker, tumble dryer and a fridge freezer. All I wanted to do now was get myself onto a detox programme and try to change my life around completely.

It was a little strange at first living on my own at my new flat and I asked Lee to stop a couple of times but he wouldn't. We were all paranoid wrecks because of doing crack, and Lee didn't want to stop, as he thought, that the police might raid the flat. I was really proud and took care of my new place. I didn't want loads of people round because it would draw attention me and I didn't want it to be seen as local doss house.

I was really settled in my flat by this point. My heroin habit and my coke habit were escalating out of control. Lee had been saying to me all week that somebody had mentioned for us to be more careful about the way we were selling the gear. I had one of my friends stop by for the night as we had been doing the crack most of the evening, so we were awake until the early hours. I had smoked nearly all my gear that night, except for a small amount that I liked to keep for when I woke up in the mornings.

The phone rang very early in the morning, but I ignored it, and switched the phone off. I went to the kitchen to get some cereal, because I was feeling hungry for once. As I got back into bed to have a smoke, I heard my front door bang very hard. I guessed straight away that it was a police knock, and I ran to the front of my flat where the kitchen was to look out of the window. The police were everywhere, and they looked up and saw me. My immediate thought was that they were busting me, so I needed to get rid of the last bit of gear I had. I would score again when they had gone. I was also thinking that if I don't hurry they would smash my door in, and that the housing association would get me thrown out. I panicked as I tried to dispose of my gear and it went everywhere: in the sink, in the bin and over the floor. I hoped the police didn't have dogs because they would certainly pick up the scent. I woke up my friend who was asleep on the settee and told him the police were at the door. Despite the panic, I opened the door casually and walked back up the stairs. The police pushed past me and darted up the stairs. There were about seven of them, mostly men and one women dressed in civilian clothes. They frantically searched my flat, and then told me that they were arresting me for intent to supply.

I tried to find out what they were going on about, but they wouldn't tell me. The woman police officer gathered up some of my clothes for me, and then after I had dressed, she put handcuffs on me. At the time I felt sure she picked the scruffiest garments she could find, but on reflection her job was to arrest me, not fit me out for a fashion parade. By this time I was in tears. One of the policemen had got my phone and was reading the message that Paul's girlfriend had sent to me, warning me that the police were on the way. Apparently they had already arrested Paul. As we left they asked where Lee was.

My addiction to heroin has led me into all sorts of trouble, and over the years I have acquired a catalogue of sins. Here was a demonstration of how easily heroin addiction can ruin your life by compelling you to do things you would not normally do. Your moral code remains intact, so you know the difference between right and wrong, but heroin blurs your ability to care, so you are not so aware of the full the impact and implications of your actions. In fact I was so careless about what I did, that it was inevitable that I would be caught.

On the way to the police station I sat in the back feeling scared and all I was thinking was what could we have done that all three of us should be arrested at the same time. My mind was in frantic turmoil in contrast to the policeman who whistled and sang, probably because in his view this was a satisfactory operation. By the time I arrived at the station I felt I was on the verge of passing out with shock. I just needed to know what I'd done and what was going to come of this? They put me into a cell and then asked me if I needed a duty solicitor (attorney) and a doctor. It began to dawn on me that this was a lot more serious than previous times when I had been arrested. This was going to mean prison and I was petrified.

The moment I sat in the cell I started to feel claustrophobic, and then panic set in, so I banged the door and rang the alarm buzzer. My stark cell was lavishly furnished with a blue plastic mattress on the floor and a toilet at the other end. Eventually somebody came and I explained that I couldn't cope in the cell and I needed to get into the outside exercise yard, se he put me out there like a dog in a kennel. As he slammed the door he turned around and said that I was going away for a long time and the he wouldn't be seeing me for a few years, with a satisfied look on his face and a sarcastic tone.

I am not usually very good with dates, but my arrest on 11th of October 2005 is engraved on my mind. I still held onto the hope that I might get out on bail or perhaps I might even get a drug treatment order. I sat on the cold floor not being able to even smoke a cigarette. It was raining and I was cold, withdrawing, and scared witless. I was thinking about my poor family and all the hard work they had put into getting my flat and making it so nice for me. What a waste: my fresh start had only lasted a month.

Once again I felt like a fourteen-year old girl wanting her mum to just come and rescue her. This time there was no chance of that. Eventually I was called in to see the doctor, and I told him that I had been on the gear for about ten years and how much I'd been using. I desperately needed something for my withdrawals, a cigarette, and I wanted to speak to my mum. After my fingerprints were taken I got to make a phone call, but my mum wasn't there so I spoke to my dad who didn't sound too sympathetic.

I returned to the cells, next to Paul and Lee, which made me feel a little better knowing that two people I cared about were close. I could hear Paul saying he was desperate for a cigarette and was quite upset, as he knew that I was smoking in the cell next to him. I was still in a deep state of shock and my medication wasn't really doing very much, because the doctor only prescribed mild painkillers, which doesn't do much for someone with a big habit.

I was called to have a chat with the duty solicitor not long afterwards. She could see that I was in no fit state for anything, but I said that I would do the police interview to get it over and done with. She advised me to say 'No comment' to all their questions. She also said that my chances of being put onto a drug treatment order were slim, and there was still the problem of my being on Probation for using my sister's credit card. So it wasn't looking good.

In the police interview I was shown a number of tapes with me selling gear to two undercover police. I kept on falling asleep which I think was due to the stress and shock of it all. Another police officer in the room asked if I needed to stop, but I carried on and got it over and done with. I gathered that I would be charged with five counts of supply. Those words hurt a lot as they said that to me and I knew I wasn't getting out of this one.

Now that I knew what the charges were I could remember how it all happened. It was a couple of months before I got my flat and Paul arranged to pick us up to go to the next town to score. I was getting into such a mess with doing the crack at this time I wanted to leave it, even though Lee and I had the money for it. Anyway, we ended up on our way to the roughest estate in town to get some crack. As it turned out we got ripped off, along with another couple. The couple then asked me if I knew where they could get gear. So I ended up giving them my phone number. The couple turned out to be undercover police, and technically this can be seen as intent to supply. I sold a couple of bags to them on a couple of occasions and Lee answered the phone once. Paul was driving at the time so he got pulled in as well.

I walked back to my cell and they must have been a bit concerned because they put me in a cell with a camera. At one point they asked if I wanted to speak to one of the counsellors, which I agreed to because it was better than being locked up constantly and not having a soul to speak to.

We had to wait until the Monday to go into the magistrate's court. In the meantime my mum came to see me in the visiting room. I gave her the biggest cuddle and we both started to cry. She told me how silly I was and that was it. I just cuddled up to her, wishing I could go home with her to be looked after. She told me to be brave and that she would come to court to see what happens. She brought me some cigarettes, some food, and Ribena drinks. Throughout everything that has happened, my family's love has never diminished despite the circumstances. Sometimes they had to be cruel to be kind. At some stage I needed to stand on my own feet and grow up, but in my present condition this was not going to happen.

I didn't realise at the time but I later found out that the police hadn't been so hard on the two boys, and Lee was even allowed his hand-held computer. I just lay there feeling ill, tired and as though my body was about to give in. I can't really remember too much whilst being in those cells because my mind was all over the place, and the trauma of it all had had a huge effect on me.

ON REMAND

On the day we were due at the magistrate's court, they moved me to a holding cell, which was even more uncomfortable than the first cell, because it just had a wooden bench. I was extremely agitated and impatient and asked repeatedly how long before I was going through. Lee and Paul were put on the male side, which also made me feel really lonely. I wanted something familiar around me, because it seemed as though my whole world was draining away.

It was hours before they called me through and I hadn't even made the effort to pull my hair back neatly. I must have looked a complete mess but the court was there to judge my offence, obviously not my looks. I just felt as though I looked like a stereotypical 'smack head' (heroin addict). I stood next to Paul and Lee in the small dock and they began to read out what evidence they had and what the charges were. I looked over to where my mum and sister Lucy were seated. The magistrates went through us one by one and asked us if we were guilty or not guilty. Lee and I pleaded guilty and Paul pleaded not guilty. We were then remanded into custody, which made me feel sick. I remember looking at Paul and Lee and their faces told me they felt the same. We were remanded for a month, and then we had to go to Crown Court for sentencing.

I was put back into the cell I was in before, and I couldn't even hear or see through the gaps in the door to see when the two boys were going. It was awful and I just sat waiting to get taken away to the unknown. Before I was picked up by the sweatbox (prison transport), I asked if I could go to the exercise yard for a cigarette. I stood out in the cold on my own still a state of shock. I had not used heroin for three days and I still could not believe where I had ended up.

I heard this familiar voice in the next yard to where I was standing. It turned out to be a girl I knew from my town, she was the girlfriend or ex-girlfriend of a girl called Michelle, a lesbian. I'd known her from when I had lived in the flat with Paul all those years ago. She told me that she was going to Peterborough prison where she said I was also heading, so I felt slightly better for knowing that at the time. She said it so casually, just like someone discussing what school they were going to or something.

Michelle lived at the other end of town to Paul and I, but I had known her for a number of years as her mum lived in the same town to where I had grown up and her brother was also a heroin addict, so like I say, you know each and every person in such a small town. She also had a habit and lived with her two young sons who were aged around one and two at the time. To my knowledge Michelle had Hepatitis C, which is a very contagious disease that is often transmitted through contaminated blood. Apparently Michelle had caught it by having unprotected sex. She was injecting at the time, and when I went to her flat I caught her kids playing with her needles like they were water pistols. What was she thinking? This was a disgusting and upsetting situation to see those poor kids at such risk.

I was handcuffed and then two officers escorted me to the sweatbox that would take me to prison. They put me into a tiny little box and locked me in. I had a small window that I could look out of, but nobody could look in. I now know how caged animals must feel. I could see people getting on to the same vehicle as we stopped at different locations and they were also being locked into their little boxes. On the way we made stops at all different courts and I could hear the other girls shouting and pleading for a smoke. I was getting increasingly worried and anxious about what was ahead of me.

When we arrived at Peterborough prison, it was already dark outside. I was escorted into the prison, where I had to wait at a desk as they put all my information onto a computer. The smell instantly reminded me of a mixture of hospitals and stale urine. They took my picture and printed it onto a card along with my prison number. The prison officers all looked serious and glum, and I didn't have anything to smile about either. I don't think I had cracked smiled for at least three days. I was completely wiped out, drained and fed up. After that I had to have a very embarrassing and humiliating strip search, and then I got to see a nurse who gave me some medication to get to sleep. She was really nice and very helpful.

I was told by one of the prison officers that my cousin was in there and she wanted to me to share a double cell with me. Sarah the girl I knew from my town pretended to be my cousin but she wasn't really. So I was taken straight to the main wing and not to the induction wing where I should have started because I was also detoxing. Every door we passed through was locked behind us, making me feel increasingly trapped. We came to the wing I was staying on, and Sarah jumped up and gave me a big cuddle, which actually made me feel a bit better.

My medication started to work as I lay on the bunk bed. My vision was becoming blurred, so I told Sarah that I felt like fainting. I was desperate to get some opiates to help with my detox and I prayed that I would get some medication the following day. I remember chatting away and the next minute I was fast asleep. I was surprised I got any sleep, but I had been given some really strong sleeping tablets. I remember that I was in and out of consciousness, that first night. I woke up all of a sudden feeling completely disorientated and unsure of where I was for a second, and then I remembered, it was prison.

The first morning we had get up early as breakfast was 7:00am and then they lock you back up at 9:00am until lunchtime if you are not working. I asked about medication, but in prisons I was quick to learn that you have to put an application in for absolutely everything. You couldn't move a muscle without a permit. My first day in prison was very strange. I felt trapped: wanting to do something but not being able to. I was panicking too because I knew that I was falling into a very deep withdrawal, and I had to wait until I was called to see a doctor in the hope of getting some medication to help me. All I wanted to do was curl up and die. I wanted it all to go away.

It is very difficult for any person who hasn't been through a detox to understand how horrendous it actually is. Most times when I have detoxed before I have taken a hot bath to relax and relieve the pains, but in prison bath times are strictly controlled. The withdrawal symptoms were bad enough, but I hated the anxious edginess even more, and this was getting worse and worse every minute. I lay on top of my covers freezing cold, fidgety and completely fed up. The stress and lack of sleep was making me crazy and I was seeing things I knew were not there: sleep deprivation had kicked in. I had no medication, no help and this was the fourth day without food. How much more could I take?

That next day they came to escort me to see a doctor. I remember sitting there on the metal bench not being able to keep still. I just looked down at my knees wishing some body would help me. My arms and legs and everything else in my body were unbearably painful. One minute I had my legs up on the bench the next they were down, I felt like smacking my head against a brick wall. I desperately wanted something to take the edge off. One of the reasons there is a high percentage of suicides and deaths in prisons is because people don't listen when the prisoner asks for help. The system is supposed to take care of the welfare of those who are locked up. Perhaps I was expecting too much of the Prison Service. Obviously it can't be designed around my individual personal needs, but even getting hold of a paracetamol was hard work in this place. The Prison Officers are there to control and keep us locked up. Other specialist authorities are supposed to care for our medical and welfare needs, but in my case they didn't seem to be well co-ordinated and it failed me.

They wouldn't even prescribe sleeping tablets or anything, even though I explained that I had some medication in the cells the previous day. I'm sure they don't employ people that have knowledge of heroin misuse because they just sent me away without a prescription. They told me that they needed to call my drugs worker outside to find out what medication I had been previously prescribed. Just because they couldn't get in touch with my detox centre they just left it. In my mixed up, paranoid and confused mental state, I felt as though I was being victimised and ignored on purpose, as if they were intent on making my suffering worse.

My crack habit just made me feel extremely tired and lacking energy for the first two days in the cells, and by now it was out of my system. The real problem was heroin withdrawal. I was in constant pain and hugely under weight (85 pounds), dehydrated and mal-nourished. Normally I would have been hospitalised and put on a drip. Did I have to collapse before I qualified for any help? I vomited one night in the cell all over the floor, and I couldn't move to even clean it up. Sarah called the staff, but because it was night time they couldn't take me down to see a nurse or a doctor. I couldn't understand why nobody could do anything and it struck me as very unprofessional. What if I had tried to take my life? Did they have a key to open my door? Would they have rushed in to help me?

Induction is a process that all new inmates have to go through. This involves filling in sheets of details and learning stuff, like where the fire exits are located. I wasn't well enough to be doing any of this because I could barely walk by myself without feeling as though I would pass out. The first week was awful. To be honest I hated the feeling of being locked in a room that I couldn't get out of because it made me panicky. This was a new feeling I had to get accustomed to, and not a particular nice one. I had no other choice. I could no longer just pop down to the shops when I wanted to, or even use the phone to call someone. I could do nothing until my door was opened for association time.

My daily routine involved; getting up for a bath and breakfast, getting locked up until lunch, being locked up again until afternoon association, and then being locked away till the early morning. I wasn't in the mood for socialising with the other people, because all I wanted to do was lay there and pray that the next day would be slightly better. Sarah had been in and out of jail since the age of sixteen so she knew a lot of the other girls in there, and in the evenings they would all come into our cell. It was horrible. I made a mistake by sharing a cell with Sarah: instead I should have been with all the other inmates who were coming off drugs on the drug free wing and were also going through the same ordeal as I was.

One day I managed to get myself to the bath that was located at the end of the wing. The withdrawal pains were driving me crazy, so I tried to drown myself and failed miserably. I foolishly mentioned it to Sarah and she told the officers, because she was concerned about me. I then had to talk to the officer about it. As a result they put me on some antidepressants that also helped me to sleep. At least they were now listening to me. I was also put on 20/52, which means they check you every 20 minutes, even during the night. There are probably thousands of people in prison that attempt suicide, but in my case I did it because I was so mentally unstable from doing such a hard detox. It is not something I would normally contemplate.

Despite my addiction I have always been a very happy relaxed person. Detoxing and the lack of sleep pushed me into doing such a stupid thing just to get them to listen to me.

My mum came up and brought me some clothes and handed it into reception. The whole time I sat with my mum on the visit she rubbed my back because my kidneys were aching so much. The officers watched us like hawks, even though my mum was a prison officer herself, but I suppose that is what they are paid for. She kind of knew how bad it must be for me because she had seen it so many times before. We didn't spend too long on her visits for the first few weeks because I couldn't sit still for too long before I needed to lie down. It was always so emotional when my mum had to leave. I must have sounded like a five year old wanting to go home with her mum. I always returned to my cell feeling horribly homesick and deflated.

I had a bit of a shock one day when my friend Brian came to visit me. It was a shock because I was still on remand, which means that people could just book in to see me and I wouldn't have a clue in advance, who was visiting. It was such a nice surprise but I really didn't know what to say to him because I was embarrassed about my situation, but he didn't judge me at all. In fact he treated me just like normal, as if we weren't even in a prison. I was really unwell on this visit so I couldn't spend more than fifteen minutes with Brian, which made me feel quite bad, as he had driven such a long way to see me. Brian is actually old enough to be my grandfather, but he doesn't look any older than my dad. I think he has a soft spot for me, because he treats me just like his other three grown up daughters, which I thought was really nice. I just wish everyone were more like Brian. He thought that I had an eating disorder or something because I was so thin and he was really concerned.

I started eating again after about three weeks and my strength began to return slowly, but I still wasn't right. I felt I needed to get out of the cell, because it was beginning to get to me, so I put an application for a job in the holistics section. This is where they teach you to do nails and massaging. It sounds like it's a bed of roses, but I assure you it isn't. The fact that it is inside prison stops it being fun, but at least I could get out and do something that I'd enjoy and I'd find relaxing.

Every time I got mail I felt happy and excited knowing somebody had taken the time to write and actually think of me. It's the same for every single prisoner. Mail is such a big thing for everyone in prison. You don't have much to look forwards to except mail and canteen. The canteen sheet would be given to us every week, and if you have money you can get little luxuries like; shampoo, toiletries, chocolate, crackers or bottles of Coke. I was told that I could earn a very small amount of money in holistics and I would also be training for a qualification at the same time. The holistics section was in the next building along with the gym, kitchens, hairdressers and a couple of other workshops.

Mass movement in the morning is where every prisoner moves from their cells to their work place. I followed like a little sheep at that stage because I didn't know anyone. I just kept my head down and got on with my business. We all waited outside in a corridor while door after door was locked behind us. Inevitably you get chatting to the other girls about what they were in for and how long had they got? In the large holistics room there were two training officers who wore what they would if they were working in a real shop; like a nurse's uniform with trousers. It was so friendly, and the relaxing music they would put on was really therapeutic. We started introducing ourselves and also went through what we would be doing like; practising doing nails on each other and also how to deal with customers. We also started learning about Indian head massage, which I found really interesting and it was something I was very good at. The officer had said to me that it would take some time to finish the course but at least I would have some certificates to take home with me.

I tried to get to know some other girls now I was feeling a little stronger, and I started sharing with a girl who worked in the servery, which came in handy because she could bring food back after dinner and lunch and my appetite was slowly returning. She lived in Oxford, and we had a lot in common because she was also in for supply. She told me that her boyfriend who was a dealer use to beat her black and blue. It was quite sad hearing her story. She told me that the first thing she wanted to do when she got out was have a pipe of crack and some gear. She had been in three years and it was coming to the end of her sentence, but after all that time I couldn't believe that she still wanted to go out and just do the same as before. I don't think she had much life to go out to, which was a shame.

Lee and Paul both sent me letters, which always cheered me up. Paul's mum put up some money to get him out on bail. Paul's mum had also been a magistrate herself so she fought to get Paul out, as she knew what she was talking about and knew the right people.

It was my birthday on the 24th of October, which meant I had been inside for thirteen days, but it already seemed like a lifetime. Looking back, it seemed like my birthdays were jinxed. I was doing a detox and had the flu' on my 21st, and now I was 24 and in prison, and I had accidentally scalded my leg with boiling water. It's not a very nice feeling to be on your own with not a soul to wish you a happy birthday and a burnt leg.

THE COUNTY COURT

After a month I had to go back to court for
sentencing. I was half living in hope that I would get
a drug treatment order and I wouldn't be returning to
prison. On the way there I looked out of the window
watching the people going to work and just getting on
with their normal lives. I then passed my little town
again and had that horrible homesick feeling in my
stomach. I hate the cells at police stations and courts
because you just get a wooden bench and nothing
else, so you just have to sit there until your called, it's
extremely uncomfortable. Finally I got called after
about an hour. I had to speak to my barrister (lawyer)
and he was totally honest with me and said that he
didn't think I was going to get a drug treatment order;
instead I would be going back to prison. If I had got

the judge who was more lenient with drug offences, then I would have had more chance, but I had got the worse judge possible. I knew things were going to be tough, so I sat there hoping I wasn't going to get a long sentence, it scared me to death.

A drugs counsellor, called Pete, who came to talk to me in the police cells, was a great guy and extremely helpful and supportive. He put a letter forwards for the judge, saying that he felt a community punishment would be much more appropriate for me as an individual and that outside help would be much more beneficial rather than a sentence in prison. I also wrote to the courts explaining how sorry I was for what I'd done and I hoped that I could get some outside treatment instead of going to prison. I don't think any of this made any difference. I don't think that the judge even read it to be honest.

I waited for about another hour before I was called into court. I looked over and saw my dad and he winked at me and smiled, my mum waved and my littler brother smiled also. My sister stuck her tongue out at me, because she always made a joke when things got a bit tense. My eldest sister couldn't make it as she had work that day, but I totally understood. I looked over the other side of the court and I could see a couple of the police that had arrested us that day. I was asked to stand and that's when the judge began to go through everything. Basically the judge reminded me that I had breeched my existing probation and this meant a custodial sentence of two years and nine months. I would serve half, and if I breeched my probation I would have to serve it all. I waved to my family and I could see my mum crying, it was really hard, but I kept my head held high as I was escorted out.

It really upset me that my best friend, Lee, got the same sentence as me, and I knew it was going to be a long time before we saw each other again. On the way back to prison I started crying as it hit home that I was going inside for quite a while and I had made a huge mess of things this time. I missed my family so much it was killing me, but I knew that I needed to put on a brave face, otherwise it would upset them on visits.

Everyday was like 'Groundhog Day' in prison, and its very mind numbing, but I knew I had to get on with it. I started to get to know a lot of the girls on the wing and I knew who to mix with and who not to. Weekends in particular really dragged by, because you had the whole day to just walk around the wing and go into other girl's cells or play pool. Most weekends I'd do other girls hair and they would do the same for me, or I would write my letters and watch TV. My letter writing was something I enjoyed doing as it made me feel a little closer to everyone I loved and cared about. I even started writing to other people in the other prisons, which made it more exciting because I received more return mail. Some days I'd get back from work and I would have about half a dozen letters to reply to, it was great and one of the few things that really made me feel good.

It was interesting listening other people's stories and what kind of nationality and background they come from. There were lots of intelligent people inside, which struck me as such a waste of talent. There were girls who had amazing voices, who were brilliant at art, or poetry, or who had amazing stories to tell.

Most people rarely think about the Criminal Justice System. As long as the police catch the criminals, and the judges put them away, and the prisons keep them locked up, then people are content to leave it that. It is only when you are confronted with the system face to face that you begin to realise that it is deeply flawed. Yes, it does do what we expect: it takes criminals out of circulation, but it does nothing to address the problem of why people become criminals in the first place. Neither is the system much good at rehabilitating prisoners, nor is it any good at preventing prisoners from re-offending. In fact it isn't even much good at telling the difference between criminals and the mentally ill.

I am not a psychiatric expert, but even I could tell that there were lots of people in prison who really should not have been inside. Instead they should have been in some kind of mental institution. They had no idea what they were saying or doing and they were incapable of looking after themselves. I mean, what were they doing in there. These people needed compassionate help: not a prison sentence.

Some of those girls were in there for the most ridiculous crimes that I felt weren't actually bad enough for a prison sentence. I just feel that there should be other ways to help people instead of just locking them up. Obviously there are very clear cases where real criminals need to be locked away to protect the general public, but in my experience there were far more cases where the public were in no danger from the girls locked up with me.

Many of the girls, like my friend Sarah, were bound to re-offend. They get institutionalised and feel they can't cope with the outside world, so they do some petty crime in order to get back inside prison, where they are more comfortable with the familiar routine. These poor people are not equipped well enough to be released, and end up caught in a vicious circle.

There are a very large huge number of people in our prisons, who are inside for drug related offences, like me. This is a huge waste of public money and prison space. Prison is not going to do any of us any good at all, because it doesn't address our problem. Surely it would make more sense to invest in more rehab centres where you are still locked up, but at the same time you have medical attention, counselling and treatment. They would also need the opportunity to take blocker medication so they feel they can adjust to leaving rehab instead of just going onto probation. Release can be a huge shock to the system, and it is very hard to adjust to the real world again. Without help, people can easily end up re-offending.

Too many prisoners don't have a home to return to after they complete their sentences so they leave with nothing and nobody. Rehabilitation services need to concentrate on these people and provide extra care, otherwise these people will almost certainly re-offend.

Finding employment is also a very big problem for people who have been in prison, including myself. Most prisoners are under-educated and lack skills, so they are already disadvantaged in the employment market, as well as having the stigma of a prison record. There is not much you can do about the prison record, other than appeal to an employer to be forgiving, but there is a lot more that could be done to help prisoners acquire skills to improve their opportunities to better themselves. People lose their motivation and confidence when they keep getting knocked back when applying for jobs. Investing in this area is much more likely to benefit ex-prisoners so that they don't have to live on welfare benefits. It is interesting that the biggest single employer in America is the Prison Service. The prisoners may be earning 'slave' wages, but at least they are learning skills and learning how to be employed.

I met a girl that I became quite good friends with called Leigh. She had lived in Norwich all her life and was inside for the same offence as me. I made fun out of her strong accent, but it didn't bother her. We actually became quite child-like, because prison makes you a little crazy and it also gets you through the day and kept us going. We would get ourselves in a complete mess when we had food fights or chucked cold water over each other while having a shower. A load of us got together and wrote her love letter as if it was from another girl and placed it under her door to wind her up. As you probably know, there are a lot of bisexuals and lesbians in prisons, so we would have a laugh and a joke with them. Even though days were extremely hard, we had to keep our spirits and sanity intact. It seemed as if every time I shared a cell with somebody, within no time they would go home because they had finished their sentence. It wasn't a nice feeling, so in the end I moved into my own cell.

I quickly put on weight and was looking a lot more like myself again. I was still on the anti-depressants for a while as I felt I needed them. Nearly everyone on my wing was on one sort of daily medication or other, which is a good indication of how mentally fragile most of us were. I met a girl who was in a very bad way, because she had set fire to herself and all her legs were extremely burnt. People don't normally do that sort of thing, so she must have been seriously disturbed. Obviously her medication didn't work for her. I also heard screaming one evening and couldn't really see a lot through the gaps in my cell door. Apparently a girl had taken one of the blades out of her razor and cut her wrists with it. This was after one of her visitors had badly upset her. When you ask for a razor in closed prisons they usually keep track of who it was issued to and when it was disposed. She had secretly taken the blade out and disposed of the actual razor. Dramas like this happened every single day.

One day I went to the library to find some books to read, and as usual I had to be escorted. Whenever we moved from one place to another we had to be escorted. There is never a minute when you are left alone, which was something I found really hard, as I like my own company sometimes. As usual there were countless doors to be unlocked and relocked as we passed through each corridor. At first this is just an irritation, but it soon drives you nuts.

There were a few incidents where girls started fighting and all the officers would run onto the wing like headless chickens, telling everyone else to get behind their doors, while they attempted to split up the fight. The girls involved would usually end up in the segregation block and losing their privileges like TV and canteen. After a while you can apply to become an 'enhanced prisoner', which makes things slightly better for you. You can spend more money on canteen and you also get more visits. I was just 'standard' at the time because I hadn't been there long enough to be enhanced.

My friend Leigh also applied for transfer to a semi-open prison, so I was hoping that if I got moved, we would both be going to the same prison. For a short while, I shared a cell with a girl called Stephanie, who was really funny, full of enthusiasm, and very intelligent. She had been in and out of prison since she was extremely young and was actually accustomed to it. Somehow, the whole prison scene didn't seem to bother her at all, but she had nowhere to go most of the time when she left prison. So in a way it was far better for her to just keep re-offending to get back to the safety and care of prison life. How sad is that?

This made me realise that there is always somebody a lot worse off than me. It is strange, but you begin to look forward to the little things and long for the normal things. I couldn't wait to be able to eat what food I wanted instead of what was served up, and to be able to take my shoes off and walk on the grass. This probably sounds odd but believe me you really start to think about things like that.

You don't get to go outside much in closed prisons, because sometimes there were not enough officers to take each wing out for exercise. I got to go out a couple of times, into a small yard with high fences all around. I remember one time close to Christmas and it was extremely cold and had started to snow. We got to go out in the exercise yard for a short while, which was so nice, even though it was freezing. One of the Indian officers took us out. Only a few of the girls off the wing came outside, and they started having a snowball fight. During the fun, the officer got a load of snow all over his turban (traditional headgear). It was hilarious, and so refreshing to be a little 'normal' for five minutes. Most of the officers don't like you doing anything enjoyable that raises a smile or makes you happy. At least that's the impression I got.

I told the officer in charge at holistics that I might get a transfer at any time to another prison. She asked me if I wanted to put a hold on the transfer so that I could finish my course. I was a little apprehensive and indecisive because I didn't know what to do, so I put off giving her an answer. The officer told me that they would give me time to decide before I would be leaving. Not long after a senior officer told me I needed to pack my things ready for a transfer to a semi-open prison at Morton Hall.

I wanted to go to a semi open more than anything, but not right at that particular time. I didn't really want to go as it was just coming up to Christmas and I didn't fancy spending it on my own with not a soul that I knew in a new jail. So I went to my friend Stephanie and the other girls, and I told them what had just happened and why I didn't really want to go at that point. One of the girls told me there was going to be another ship-out after Christmas anyway. All the girls told me refuse, but if you refuse a direct order it invites trouble. At that stage I didn't think about the possible trouble, all I wanted was to stop where I was. I knew things were going to be extremely difficult for me over Christmas, and I needed some friends around me at least. I couldn't believe, and still can't believe what I did next, just because I didn't want to go on that ship-out to another prison.

The girls all stood around me telling me to strip off and put cocoa butter over myself so they wouldn't be able to make me get on the sweatbox. I looked at them in amazement at what they were saying, but it made sense afterwards. It was Stephanie who jumped in first and stripped off. She had no shame whatsoever. She told me to do the same otherwise they would do it for me. I had no choice, so I stripped down to my knickers and put this cocoa butter all over me. It was like baby oil in a way, and it is extremely difficult to grab hold of anyone with that stuff all over them.

The officer must have had the shock of his life when I walked over to the door of my cell. He opened the flap on the door and then shut it as quickly as he had opened it. I shouted through the door that I didn't want to go and told him my reasons too. The officers reacted by putting the whole prison on lock-down. I could hear the officers telling the girls to get behind their doors and I could also hear a few of them getting mad. Most of them had no idea why they had to get locked up instead of going to their work place, so they started kicking the doors and shouting. My cell then got locked as well so Stephanie and I sat waiting until we knew for certain that they weren't going to put me in that sweatbox.

The senior officer came back after about half an hour and told me I had to go. He was getting quite mad by this time because I was still refusing. I tried to cover myself up, even though Stephanie just sat there on show with no shame at all. He demanded to know if I was refusing to obey a direct order, and I said that I certainly was. I don't think he expected me to be so determined. After about half an hour he came back to tell me that I didn't have to go, but because I had refused a direct order they would have to review what further action they might take. Stephanie was told to go back to her cell and I was locked in mine until further notice.

She really saved me that day, but it wasn't too nice for the next couple of days, because I had to stop in my cell and not come out for association or work. It was horrible, but I'd succeeded and I wasn't going anywhere thank God, well not straight away anyway. The following day I received a letter saying I had to go to the adjudicator (prison judge) after refusing a direct order. An officer escorted me to the next building where I would be adjudicated. I had to wait in a large holding cell where Stephanie joined me. She didn't seem at all worried, but I was concerned that my defiance might affect my getting a tag and early release.

I was on my best behaviour, because I'm not really a menace to society. Perhaps I do stupid things sometimes without thinking before hand, but I've always been like that. Obviously I still have some growing up to do. Stephanie came out smiling and told me not to worry, so I walked into this small room and looked straight at the prison judge and three other officers. The judge told me to take a seat and to explain why I had refused to go to the semi-open prison. He seemed to be a very nice reasonable guy so I told him that I was extremely worried, because my dad couldn't travel far as he was just about to have an operation on his knee. Which wasn't a complete lie. Actually my dad would have asked his girlfriend to drive him. Fortunately my excuse worked, and I was told not to get into any more trouble for the next 3 months otherwise I would lose all my privileges and maybe more.

Prison does funny things to you and often makes you do stuff you usually wouldn't do. Even now I wouldn't get to finish the holistics course, so I just learnt as much as I could before the New Year.

This was my first Christmas without my family. I remember it as clear as anything; we played silly games on the wing and the officers had brought in chocolates as prizes. It wasn't what I call fun, but I had no other choice than to make the most of the situation.

New Years Eve was a surreal experience. We all got locked up at 8:00pm, probably because they were so short of staff. What a way to spend New Years Eve locked in a cell, and then suddenly at midnight the prison went wild. Everyone started shouting happy New Year and began to start kicking their doors; we could also hear the guys on the men's side doing the same. It was quite a buzz considering the circumstances and amazing how much noise came from the prison.

SEMI-OPEN PRISON

After the New Year I would be going onto the next prison. I was kind of looking forwards to the change, because spending time in the same place doing the same tiresome things can really start to get you down, so you need to break it up a bit by moving and having a change. I was pleased because I knew that Leigh was also going to the same place, so at least I would a friend there. I had to pack all my clothes into prison bags, and then I popped around saying goodbye to the few people I had made friends with including Stephanie. She told me she would write and send me some money, which was very sweet. A lot of people usually say that they will keep in touch, but they don't. However, Stephanie did keep in contact.

I remember going to Morton Hall on the 4th January 2006. It took about an hour and a half to get there and it was a very uncomfortable ride and very hot. I hadn't seen the outside world for a while, so I was looking out of the tiny little window at the world going by. By the time we arrived I was dying for the toilet, but it wasn't as though I could just jump off and go, so I had to wait. We were at the gates for at least 20 minutes so I shouted to the driver and she told me she would try and hurry things as much as she could. The big gates were locked behind us as we pulled up besides a small reception building. The whole place reminded me of an army camp.

There were girls just wandering around, which seemed quite strange at first, as I'd got use to seeing everyone being locked behind doors. There was only one big fence that went around the whole perimeter of the prison. Eventually we were asked to get off the sweatbox and to sit in reception while our bags taken through to reception. I got to use the toilet, and it seemed really bizarre that I could use a toilet like you would anywhere else. Leigh asked if we could be on the same wing together as we didn't know any other girls. There were two African girls on our sweatbox, who told us the prison was actually a prison for foreign nationals. We literally walked through one gate and there we were inside the semi-open prison. It felt so odd that we were just wandering around with hardly any officers in sight.

It didn't seem as bad as closed jail at first and I found out they called the buildings 'units' instead of 'wings'. The first unit we stayed in was called Windsor. We were only due to stay there a short while until they found us a permanent place. The units reminded me of large bungalows that had long corridors that lead to the cells. Morton Hall was more like a disused army camp: old and worn, whereas Peterborough was brand spanking new and really made you feel as though you were in prison. Peterborough had only been going for a short time, which is probably why I think it was being run so badly.

Leigh and I had cells next to each other. I felt better knowing that I had somebody to talk to. I am always uneasy in new surroundings and I felt even worse at Morton Hall because I was so far away from my family.

The rooms (cells) were a lot different, inside it was all in pine and the TV was in a wooden box on the wall. There were two small wardrobes and a door to a shower, toilet and sink. I looked out of the window, which was actually a glass window. It felt strange because the windows at the closed prison were small with a little vent. I unclipped the window and pushed the top open, as if I was letting in some freedom instead of fresh air. These cells were actually slightly different to the ones we were to get moved to later on, as they had there own bathroom and shower joined on.

I could see fields surrounding the prison, where girls were walking a few goats. Leigh told me that there was a farm where prisoners could work, and I told her about my experiences at the stables. We both commented how strange it felt to walk about without having an officer with you all the time.

I wanted to speak to my mum, but my phone credit had not been transferred yet, so Leigh and I went exploring. Just around the corner from our rooms there was a poolroom, with a stereo player. Leigh had some CDs so we listened to those while we played pool. There were some other new girls there, but they were all from different countries and didn't speak much English.

In the closed prison we ate in small groups, whereas Morton Hall had a large dining hall where they fed about five hundred. On the way to dinner we were not allowed to walk on the grass, which I suppose is reasonable considering 500 people were using the route. The hall wasn't that busy when we arrived as we were the last unit to get called and everyone else had eaten. Normally there was a choice of three different main meals at night and the same at lunch times, which we could order what we wanted in advance. At night we were handed a carrier bag with bread, a couple of butters, tea bags, coffees, a few sachets of sugar, and a small carton of milk. We were told we could only make toast in the morning if we were on the 'enhanced' unit.

Luckily my dad had been sending me some money every couple of weeks because it would take a week before I got paid from any job I did in this new prison. I thought about the farms, but the weather was so on and off I didn't really fancy it. There were other workshops where you washed and dried clothes or packed laundry, and then there was education, kitchens, gardens or gym orderly. I had already put on some weight and I needed some fitness to hold it all together, so gym orderly was a natural choice for me.

After a sleepless night I went to the gym with Leigh. We were told what kind of sports we could do and times what times we were allowed in the gym. I asked about being the gym orderly and another girl called, Kay, said that she wanted to do that as well. Later, I was moved on to another unit called, Sharmen and my friend Leigh moved next door to me.

My working day started at 7:20 am with a shower and breakfast and then I started start doing a bit of cleaning at the gym at 8:00am. I had to sign people into the gym and show them how to use the different equipment. I had a personal workout too most days. After lunch, it was back to the gym for more training. I was doing an NVQ certificate in fitness and by the end of it I would have a few qualifications to take with me.

Basically there were three different types of prisoners; the un co-operative ones who didn't want to work and were always in trouble and were usually on 'basic' with no privileges, and then there were people like myself who had just got themselves into a bad situation and knew it was the first and last time in prison, and finally the ones that were institutionalised and just didn't care about anything.

Some days were good and some days were bad, but mostly good. I felt human again after going through such a dreadful detox. I still had heroin in my mind most days for at least the first six months. Some days we played silly little pranks on each other like; throwing cold water on other girls while they were in the bath or we would have food fights. We actually acted like school kids again, but it was for our sanity because there wasn't anything else that made you smile or laugh. The important thing was to keep your nose clean, because even the silliest things went into your record file, and this could affect your date for early release tags.

I felt so sorry for the foreign nationals because they get given a date when their sentence is over, but then have to wait for a deportation flight date which can take anything up to 6 months more. It must have been frustrating for them because they rarely, if ever, got to see their family and then on top they have to do longer than their sentence. I made a friend with a girl from Malaysia, who was doing 6 months for credit card fraud and she ended up doing much longer.

I increased my body weight by about 50 percent, and the daily exercise kept me toned and fit. For the first time in years I looked like a real person instead of a shadow, and I had good reason to feel good about myself. I think that everyone puts weight on in prison: you eat because there is nothing else to do.

Being able to phone home was extremely important, and having postage stamps and writing paper meant the world to me. Receiving mail was another highlight of the day. My friend Brian wrote to me every single week and often sent me flowers. Flowers made my day for a week. Weekends were really boring even though my family would take it in turns coming up to visit; My mum and sister one week and then my dad and his girlfriend another week. My friend Brian also came up with my mum sometimes in the week. To be honest, I preferred not to have too many visits as it made feel homesick and deflated afterwards. It was a horrible feeling not being able to go home with the people you love most. Obviously it always makes you feel so much better knowing you've got someone who wants to see you, but it's not so nice afterwards.

My friend Leigh had children, but because she had such a bad time with drugs they were taken away and lived with her family and didn't come up to see her very often. It was so sad to see the pain in her face, and she often told me that she wanted to build bridges with her family again.

Heroin had nearly destroyed everything in my life and I nearly lost my family too. I don't know what would have done without them, but thankfully they have forgiven me for the terrible mistakes I made in the past.

At weekends I would sit and write my letters with my music on, and just concentrated on what I wanted to do when I got out. I made friends with a lot of the girls from different countries on the unit, and I learnt a lot about their cultures. It was really funny what kind of things we missed inside. Like me, most said they missed their family. The second most popular thing was food. A lady from Nigeria said it was a certain type of soup. I didn't miss soup, but it made me realise that we really do take a lot of things for granted. Sometimes, if I went to the toilets at night I would meet a large Jamaican lady bathing herself from the sink rather than using the bath. I thought it was strange, but if that is what she was accustomed to, who am I to argue with culture?

Morton Hall was a bit like the TV show, Big Brother, because there are cameras everywhere you went. On the other hand we had a high degree of freedom. We could even sit outside and sunbathe if it was hot. I would just lie there and pretend that I wasn't in prison and try to imagine that I was on some lovely tropical beach. It was something that kept my mind off of everything and also helped me with my panic attacks and stress levels. I was up and down really about how I felt in prison, but the worst thought was that something would go wrong outside with my family or friends, and I couldn't do anything about it.

I started a four-day course at the gym doing a first aid, which I thought would be a good qualification. I had to learn how to bandage, how to cope in an emergency with somebody who is badly injured, and how to give mouth-to-mouth resuscitation. I was also trying to keep myself focused and busy on the gym course which would also gave me a few certificates, but it is sometimes very hard to concentrate when you feel low and not completely happy. I don't really think that people truly understand how stressful it is inside, particularly when you have just done a rapid detox, and you are missing your family. It can really drag you down, hearing all the girls talking about negative things at times. It comes to the point where you go to your cell and shut your door so you can't hear any more.

I was feeling really positive about staying off heroin and everything else. In fact when anybody spoke about doing drugs, I would just walk away. It was my way of coping with it. Doing drugs was the last thing I wanted to talk about or hear. Despite my determination and resolve, my mental state was still very fragile and it didn't need much to tip me over the edge. Out of the blue, I had some bad news. I remember it was a weekend and I was in my cell, when I had a knock on the door and an officer asked me to go to the chapel. This was a standard routine for breaking bad news, as if it would have less impact coming from the ladies in the chapel. The chaplain asked me to take a seat and not to worry too much. She had a message from my mother saying that my sister had been arrested. I felt my face turn pale as she told me and I knew that it had to be something to do with my sister working as an officer in a male prison. I guessed that it was to do with drugs because I couldn't think of anything else. I tried to call my mum but there was no reply, so I sat with Leigh, wondering what could have happened. My sister had never been in trouble in her life. I was always the one classed as a black sheep. What had she done and what was going to happen to her?

Eventually I got hold of my sister and she cried down the phone to me. She sounded a complete wreck and I felt sick as she explained what had happened to her. She told me that a guy in the prison had put her under a lot of pressure and told her if she didn't bring some drugs in for him then I would be stabbed by somebody in my prison. I couldn't believe that she had been so silly and not told anyone about this. I felt really sad for my sister and her little boy because they were the ones who were going to suffer. This guy had put my sister in a terrible position and she was too scared to say no apparently. I can't say that this was the complete truth as I wasn't there, but this was what she told me.

I felt so sorry for her, because I knew that this would mean a prison sentence. It was the last place I wanted her to go. I sat back in my cell thoroughly depressed, wondering what else was going to go wrong. I felt so down that I reached out for comfort and support from heroin.

Some of the girls inside were using Subutex (an opiate based medication). If this is used when you have been off heroin for some time, then it has more or less the same effect as heroin. I snorted some Subutex and half an hour later started getting the effects from it. I actually looked like someone on heroin, my eyes were pinned and I felt my energy return, and I was relaxed and warm, but most of all the stress and worry disappeared. One of the girls on the unit 'grassed us up' (reported us) to the officers for using Subutex. They only had a heroin test kit at the time.

If you tested positive for heroin (Class A) you were given extra days on your sentence. Subutex was only Class B so you didn't get extra days added on. The governor promptly had Subutex test kits sent in and before I knew it I was taken to the sample room to be tested. My results were positive so I got sent down the block (punishment block) and I started to cry when they locked me in the cell with nothing except a radio, my writing paper, a pen and a book.

I was distraught and upset with myself because I had been so stupid in a moment of weakness, and had made matters even worse for myself. As a result I was put on closed visits, which meant I would be behind glass and couldn't cuddle or kiss my family. That was the hardest part because they would have to sit behind a glass screen so that you couldn't touch or make physical contact and you couldn't hear each other very well. I felt that it was unfair on my family. In effect they were being punished as well as me. I was down the block for a whole week, and had all the time in the world to think and worry about it. Not being able to talk to anyone for a whole week was horrible. Why had I been stupid and got myself in that situation? I was so angry with myself, and thought about flushing the tablets that I had left down the toilet. I argued with myself, trying to decide whether to throw it away. Eventually, common sense prevailed and I flushed it away. I was so pleased I done it that I even wrote to my mum about it. It was extremely boring and lonely with nobody to speak to. It made think long and hard about how stupid I had been. That week felt like the longest week in the world, and by the end I had also run out of cigarettes.

When I returned back to the unit all the girls greeted me, which was nice, but a bit too much at first. There were too many people around me, so I went back to my cell to get myself together. When I looked in the mirror I was horrified. Down the block I had lost my appetite, so I looked awful; pale, thin in the face and my eyebrows were in need of drastic attention. The girls told me that another couple of them were due to go down there for positive urine tests, so I felt slightly better knowing that I hadn't been victimised by being the only one who was punished.

So I carried on with all my courses and was becoming more and more anxious about my tag date (early release) coming up. I was praying that I would get out after having my small relapse, and I hoped that it wouldn't count against me. Leigh's date came and she was told she was going home, I was really pleased for her but was going to miss her dreadfully. We had done our whole sentence together and we had said we would keep in touch, as she only lived an hour and a half away from me.

My other friend was Kay, at the gym was also due out soon. We had a lot of very funny times together. We were both gym orderlies, so we would secretly put the sauna on and nip in it at weekends for twenty minutes. How we got away with it I'll never know. We were like naughty schoolgirls stealing a little bit of illicit luxury. It also did us the world of good. Nobody in prison had such well cared for skin as us.

The girls, who I had taken Subutex with, did a cruel and spiteful thing to my Malaysian friend, which was the last and final straw as far as I was concerned. They asked my friend Yu, to write a letter to the boyfriend of one of these girls. Apparently she was forbidden to make contact with him, which is why she wanted Yu to write the letter. Unknown to Yu, they put a Subutex tablet in with the letter. An officer found the tablet and it was blamed on Yu, so she was sent down the block too. The poor girl was devastated. She was being punished for being gullible, so I no longer spoke to those girls after that.

I sat in my cell on a weekend writing my letters on my own when one of the girls who had been in for five years ran past the door crying her eyes out. She had been told that she had done six months longer than she should have, so she was ordered to pack her things and get out of the prison immediately. I couldn't imagine how much of a shock this must have been. She had no time to prepare herself, and no family either, so she would have to find a hostel to live in. The poor girl didn't want to go and was crying because she was so scared about leaving. How was that poor girl going to cope? This was just another example of how the prison system doesn't work. It's really sad to think somebody would rather stay in prison than get out.

I tried to put in for a town visit because I was also quite apprehensive about getting out. I needed some practice at doing normal things after a year inside locked away from ordinary life: no cars, no interaction, no bills, and no handling money. It was too scary to think about. I was refused a town visit and was told that I should just concentrate on my tag.

The fact that I didn't get a town visit worried me even more. I was called to the main office to have a chat with the governor, which made me even more nervous, because he didn't usually ask for private meetings about tags. For people like me, getting an early release tag was the ultimate goal and hugely important, whereas the prison staff thought of it more like a game. We were given our tag dates right at the beginning, but it had to be confirmed or delayed by the governor. At least I got a chance to have my say, and I told him that I had a job to at my dad's work place hopefully. He joked about my accent and then told me I'd find out soon enough.

A couple of weeks later I was walking to the gym when I bumped into the governor. I was worried and impatient because I only had three days to go before my tag date. He asked me if I had been notified of my tag date and I told him I hadn't. He kept me in suspense for what seemed like ages while my heart was beating like crazy, and then he gave me the good news. My face must have lit up like bright red Christmas lights, as I ran off towards my wing to call my mum to share the great news. I ran as fast as I could, crying my eyes out with joy and excitement. I can't describe how happy and overjoyed I felt. I was on cloud nine.

I couldn't wait to tell my mum, and I spoke so fast that she didn't quite catch what I said at first, so I had to repeat myself, as I cried with sheer happiness. I couldn't think about anything else apart from the fact that I was going home and that was all that mattered. I think my mum was worried because she knew that I would be returning home and that I would be exposed to all those temptations again. For the next couple of days I just thought about home and how things were going to be this time round. It was all positive stuff like; making a lot of good changes this time for the best, and not going back down the road I had been down for many years.

The day before I was going home I had to pack my things and take them to the reception. My room looked so bare when I had taken all my pictures and cards down. I felt sick with apprehension and had no idea how I was going to feel when I walked through the gates and saw my sister, my dad and my brother. I think there was so much adrenalin rushing around my body that I wouldn't sleep very well that night. Everyone on the wing knew I was going home the next day and people that I'd known for the whole time said that they would miss me. I didn't sleep at all well because the thought of being so close to freedom again gave me itchy feet.

FREEDOM

After a morning shower I got myself ready to leave what I'd called home for a year. I wanted to look my best, even though I hadn't got much to wear, but I did my hair and make up. I was called earlier than expected and everyone on the unit came to say goodbye. I was getting out and that's what mattered. The officers put all my things into bags to take with me and handed me back my rings that I hadn't worn for a year. It felt great when I put my Nan's ring onto my finger and it also made me think about how much I was looking forwards to wearing earrings again and clothes of my own choice again because I felt such a mess being in prison. In no time the officers told me that my dad had arrived. My heart was in my mouth and I had clammy hands from feeling nervous. As I walked out and saw my family I felt overwhelmed. Everyone cuddled me as I got into the car. It felt so strange because we only said a few words to each other on the way back and I just sat there quietly gathering my thought and trying to get accustomed to being out in the open.

Before I knew it I could see the signs for my town again, it had been a year since I had drove passed in the sweatbox on the way to prison. It felt so much longer than a year, but it was a good feeling to be home again. My sister took me to her house so I could get my self ready to go to the pub for a welcome home drink. I went to the pub and sat nervously at the bar. It all felt very strange seeing people getting on with their day-to-day lives. I had missed life on the outside so much. My mind was so set on staying off the gear and moving forwards and I felt so positive too. After a few more drinks I started to feel a little bit more relaxed. A few people in the pub knew that I had just got out of prison and they all wished me luck.

I had to be back to the house for 3:00 pm because the tagging people were due any time after that to put the tag on my ankle. One of my friends, who I used to go around with in my clubbing days, was coming to the house to have some drinks with me, so I was really looking forwards to seeing her and having a normal evening at home. It was such a relief to be out of that prison. I had to keep myself together though because one of the rules on my licence sheet was to not be drunk when the tagging officers arrived. I hadn't had a drink for over a year, so it affected me extremely quickly. Anyway, they arrived at 7.00 pm and put my tag put on. They were very nice and not at all judgmental even though they knew I had been drinking. They explained that I needed to be in by 7:30 pm every evening otherwise it would be considered that I had breeched my tag licence. I also had to walk to the bottom of the garden because they had to make sure the tag wouldn't go off if I popped outside for a cigarette.

I also had to report to probation every week, so that probation could ask me how I was getting on. This was also part of my licence. My plan was to get myself a job, but at the same time I needed to get adjusted to being out of prison, which I don't think anyone truly understood. I didn't realise how hard things were going to hit me when I come out, but after a week things really did. I found it so hard to walk down the street on my own in case I bumped into any of my old acquaintances. I remember looking out of the window with butterflies in my stomach not knowing where to go or who to go and see for company. All my old friends were heroin addicts and I just didn't want to risk anything. I sat having an argument with myself: whether or not to see an old friend that lived around the corner.

I decided on visiting her and went around her house where there were a couple of old faces I new, Angie and Levi had both been to prison so they both new exactly how I was feeling. We decided on a visit to the pub, but I was so nervous about doing anything, or seeing anybody, that I felt I needed something to boost my confidence before going out to see the people I hadn't seen in such a long time. I think I instantly felt all the old reminders being around two old acquaintances and this put thoughts in my head that were going to cause more problems again. So I went up to Angie's toilet and sniffed some Subutex. Within about fifteen minutes the Subutex started to work and I didn't feel as worried. I know you must be thinking 'how could I be so utterly foolish to expose myself to temptation'? Surely I knew that I couldn't resist? I know I was kidding myself, but at the time I convinced myself that I wouldn't slip back into the world of heroin, because Subutex contained a blocker (like Naltrexone) which meant I couldn't use heroin. I felt so guilty when we went down to the pub because as I walked in it felt as though they were staring right at me, as if they knew what I had done. I felt completely 'out of it' and I sat at the pub hardly able to keep my eyes open. I felt really angry with myself. Why did I have to always turn to drugs? Why couldn't I just be normal? What chance did I really have?

This was the first time I had ever lived with my dad and his girlfriend and I actually was looking forwards to getting to know him. But it soon became apparent that this was going to be extremely difficult living with him because I couldn't even go to the toilet without him wanting to know what I was doing. I know he was worried about me, which I could understand, but it wasn't long before we started arguing about ridiculous little things. I felt like I was being bullied all the time. I'd lived on my own since I was sixteen years old and I'd fended for myself. I couldn't cope with having to tell my dad and his girlfriend where and what I was doing. They would ask me in the same way that you would treat a ten-year old child.

Needless to say, I started going off the rails again, and before I knew it I was an addict again. When was this nightmare going to end? Heroin had taken everything from me, but I still couldn't help myself. It is all I had known since a teenager and however much I tried it always beat me. I longed for a normal life, a job, a nice house, and maybe even marriage. Just when my sister and my mum needed me most, I had turned to heroin again. I admitted it to my mum and my sister, but I couldn't tell my dad. He just couldn't understand how difficult it was for me, how fragile I felt when left prison. I did tell my good friend Brian because I knew he would be more sympathetic and understanding.

They say that heroin dulls your emotions, but I still felt an awful lot of guilt about messing up again. Regardless of the consequences, addiction sits at the back of your mind forever, waiting for an opportunity to strike again. I suffer from self-delusion like most addicts; I kid myself that I will just have some today and that will be it, because tomorrow I will stop. I say this to myself almost every day, and at the time I sincerely believe it, but in practice it never happens. Maybe addiction changes the way we think, I'm not sure, but I know it takes a very long time to learn to resist and I don't think you fully recover for the rest of your life. I know it takes me about two months to detox with medication, and I don't feel mentally stable and physically better until I have been off treatment for about a year afterwards. I know it's extremely difficult for non-addicts to comprehend all of this but this is exactly how addiction works.

In my particular case, my mental state is relatively fragile. If I get stressed, then my mental balance is upset and I immediately feel unable to cope. Even simple things like arguments are enough to upset me. As a family we were going through an awful ordeal with my sister and it worried me to death and unbalanced me. I lost all my confidence, my drive and self-respect. I felt lost, so I turned to heroin, the only thing that I know would make things better.

My dad helped me with starting my driving lessons again. It was an ambition that I really wanted to do and get finished. I knew that if I wanted to get myself a job I would need to have a car so I could get to work. Public transport where I live is virtually non-existent. My sister had been told that she was definitely getting a prison sentence, because she had been in a position of trust and it was seen as very serious. So she said I could have her little car. My dad told me that a girl I use to go to school with worked at an opticians, and that I could probably get a job there too. I knew I hadn't been in work for a long time and I was pretty sure I that my prison record would make it hard to find a job. Despite this, I decided to give it a shot.

On the day of my first interview for the job, I dressed myself very smartly because I wanted to make a stunning first impression, and I took my new, professional up-to-date C.V. with me, that my friend Brian created for me on his computer. I had already prepared the ground by writing a letter to them honestly explaining my circumstances. At this first interview I was in a room full of other ladies, who made me nervous but I was determined and I meant business. I told the panel that I'd done a little bit of agency work, which I did when I first come out of prison for a short time. We also had to do a little exam, which I felt I could have done better at if I had concentrated more. Maybe having a smoke before I walked in didn't help matters. To my surprise I was then called for a second interview.

The second time, the interview was with two managers in a small room. They asked me a few questions, and told me they would let me know the result. On my way home I had a call from them saying the job was mine. I couldn't believe that I got the job, particularly when I had been up against so many other ladies with better qualifications. Strangely, this victory did nothing to boost my confidence, although I still know that I can make a good impression when I need to. My dad was so happy that I'd finally got myself a job that included training and had long-term career prospects.

My sister was due to appear before the Crown Court and we all went to support her and pray that she would be treated leniently. It was a bad sign that she had the same judge that I had. Karla got sentenced to four and a half years in prison, which was a crushing blow for her and all of us. I couldn't get my head around the fact that my sister was going to end up in prison. This was something that I never thought would happen. My family had put up with such a lot with me ending up in prison, and now it was happening all over again with my sister, but a lot more difficult because Karla had a little boy. She had made a terrible mistake, and it put her in a place she really didn't belong. However we all knew that she was strong and that she would cope like I had. Sometimes these situations make us a lot stronger or they break us, and I knew that Karla would hold her head high and survive. What had happened to our family? Once we had seen such happy times. What had we done to deserve all this?

I had my driving theory test before I started my job but I kept failing. In the end it took me four attempts before I finally passed, and phoned my dad to let him know. I think that drugs probably impaired my ability to study the Highway Code, but I have never been much good at academic study. It was a great boost to my self-esteem to finally achieve something.

I started the job along with five other trainees, and soon got to know the job. I was doing so well and enjoyed doing it. I was working directly with the general public advising and selling spectacles. There were so many different things to do in one day and that's what I liked about it: it kept me busy and it wasn't boring. I learnt about different types of lenses and many other features about spectacles that I didn't even know existed. We had a sales bonus system and sometimes I was the top earner, which I was very proud of because I had only just started.

The only problem was I needed to get off the heroin again which was going to be really hard. I kept falling ill or I was withdrawing and had to have time off. I think the drugs and working full time made me run down.

There was a lot of competition between the sales team so I was under a lot of pressure too. The stress made me even more paranoid to the point where I thought the others were conspiring against me or looking down their noses at me. I also felt that I was always being watched because they knew my history. I just wanted to be treated like everybody else. Things weren't the same any more and I began to lose interest in the job. I got to the last level of training but all that hard work was ruined when I was called into the office and was told that I no longer had the job. I was really upset, although to be fair I did have a lot of days off when I was unable to score my gear. I could have been an extremely good sales dispenser but being an addict proved I that could not hold a job down.

I failed my first driving test during the time I worked at the opticians so I immediately booked a second test. The first time, I had a female testing me, but the second time I had a male. I really thought that there was no way I was going to pass because he wouldn't even make conversation and kept on telling me off for speaking. This made my nerves even worse. The whole way through the test I was sweating profusely while trying to remember to use my mirrors in an obvious fashion. Suddenly somebody pulled out in front of me so I had to slam my breaks on sharply. I think this showed him that I was a safe driver and I could see he looked impressed at this point. At the end of the test he told me I was just two points away from failing but I had passed. I was so happy that I was nearly in tears. Nothing could beat how good I felt that day.

My dad put my sisters car in his local garage to fix a few small mechanical things, and then he taxed and insured it for a year. I waited impatiently for the documents to arrive. Finally I would able to drive on my own for the very first time. I was a little nervous without anyone sitting next to me but it felt so good. I couldn't wait to show somebody because I loved my little car and having the independence it gave me.

I was now twenty-six years old and I didn't have a lot to show for it. It was time to get my act together. I felt sick to the stomach that I was actually killing myself with this terrible drug. It's an illness in itself, but nothing like having cancer or a terminal condition. It made me feel ashamed. Once again I knew I had to stop. We all have choices, but for me the hardest part is the thought of facing another detox, and knowing that all the pain and suffering would be wasted if I couldn't stay off.

EGYPT

It wasn't long before I decided that I had to get out of dad's house because it was too stressful, so I went and lived with my friend Brian. It was like heaven being in a house where I wasn't being told what to do and asked where I was going every five minutes. Brian knew about my addiction, but that was my business and he didn't judge me for it. Brian was so patient and tolerant with me, and treated me with such loving care and affection, just like my Nan. He just wanted to see me off drugs. Things were a lot calmer with me being in a position where I could do as I pleased. I couldn't cope with my dad dictating what I did in my life, I knew he cared, but he just did things completely the wrong way at times and I couldn't take all his crap.

While I was staying at Brian's place I didn't realise how fortunate I was. I had it made. He was so kind and generous and it didn't cost a penny. He even did my washing, and sometimes the ironing too. He also made sure that I ate regularly and would cook for me at any time, day or night. I could come and go as I pleased with no questions asked. Foolishly I didn't use my guardian angel to help me detox and stay off heroin. Looking back, I am sure his kindness and strength would have been exactly what I needed to have kept clean.

Over the next two years and three months I visited Karla every so often with my mum. She went to exactly the same prisons that I went to, so I knew exactly how she was feeling except she obviously missed her little boy as well. Luckily he had a great dad who he lived with while she was away. Time seems to drag by when you are in prison; every minute feels like five, and every hour feels like forever. You have so much time to think and regret being there. Karla's boyfriend stuck by her the whole time until she was released. She was very lucky to have a very supportive partner. After her release, Karla moved straight in with Liam and later that year in 2010 he proposed to her.

My mum invited me for a holiday to Egypt for two weeks and I jumped at the chance, but I knew I would have to detox and stabilise myself on methadone (an opiate based medication) while I was away. This would be yet another chance to stop. I was extremely worried about going because once I was there I would have to get on with it however ill I felt. I wouldn't be able to just nip off and go to a local dealer for some heroin. The day before my mum and I were due to leave, I borrowed some money from a female friend and bought a small amount of gear to take with me. Yes, I know I was crazy because I had no idea what the penalties were for drug trafficking in Egypt. It could have been a life sentence, or even death for all I knew. What was the point in taking this risk, when I was going to stop any way? The thought of having to get on that plane with no gear scared the life out of me. This wasn't stupidity: it was monumental stupidity. Clearly, addiction robs you of all logical reason. Naturally I was paranoid and panicking about having the gear on me. I was praying I wouldn't get stopped because I suspect that my mum would have been in trouble too. To be honest I was crapping myself, but just for once the angels were on my side. Even now I cannot believe I did it.

I had it hidden in a condom and concealed inside my body. I was desperately worried because I though it might open up or even get stuck. Once I arrived I was desperate to use some gear, as it had been many hours since I had last used, so I admitted what I had done to my mum. She was furious which is completely understandable. My next challenge was to get some tin foil, so I asked my mum for some money to walk down to the local shop within the hotel. After a lot of searching I finally found a roll of foil and ran back to the room to have some gear. Once I had finished my gear over the next few days, I began to just use my methadone that had been prescribed. I wasn't feeling great, but I managed. It was better detoxing away from danger and with medication than previous times when I had nothing to help me. I think being able to cut down made such a difference to how I felt over that holiday period.

During that holiday I met a young guy called Luke. I was more than a little attracted to him. I suppose I was vulnerable and I was on holiday, so it seemed perfectly natural. We spent most of the holiday together and with his family. I was keen to continue our relationship after we returned and arranged to go to his house in Coventry. While we were in Egypt everything was very romantic, but as soon as he got back he changed completely. He virtually ignored me during my visit, which made me feel rejected and depressed. At least I was depressed at first, but later this changed to fury. I was so indignant that he had treated me in such a deplorable manner. It was so ill mannered and immature. Personally I think he had another girlfriend and our holiday romance was just a fling as far as he was concerned, which is not how I saw it. I was spitting fire. This affair upset me so much that I went back to heroin almost immediately.

Months went by and I was still struggling with gear and feeling quite down after having felt I had finally met somebody who I thought could have had a huge impact in changing my life. He had treated me so badly that it had stayed with me for quite a while afterwards. I needed something to cheer me up and snap me out of it.

One day I sat with Brian and mentioned about wanting a new car because I knew Karla's car was old, and eventually my sister might want the car I back once she got out. So I asked if he would lend me the money to get a new one and he said he would. So I started looking in various car magazines until I eventually found one that really stood out. It was a racing green 'Clio' with 17 inch alloy wheels. It had been in a previous accident and the air bag had deployed, but that didn't stop me going to have a look. I asked my friends Rob and Lee to come along with me, as Rob is a mechanic and could check it over for me.

Brian transferred the money to my account and off we went. When we arrived we pulled up to quite a large new estate and the lady told us that car belonged to her nephew, which he had crashed a couple of times. He sounded like a bit of a boy racer who drove recklessly, so they took the car away from him. I went for a test drive in it and immediately fell in love with it. It needed a new steering rack, so Rob suggested that I should beat the price down a bit. Eventually we made a deal. We chatted away and got on so well that she mentioned she was going to get her nails done in the next town, and I said that I needed mine doing too. As it turned out I got my nails done and bought a car at the same time.

It wasn't long after my holiday that I spoke to one of my old friends. He lived around the corner when I was five years old, and was someone I confided in and also spent some time with occasionally. He also was on the gear but hadn't started until he was 22 years old, so he was a relative newcomer. Andrew was a year older than me and has a great voice. I remember when I was a young girl hearing him sing from my garden. To be truthful, his magical, powerful singing voice doesn't match his general appearance: he just belts it out like a guy with twice his build. Anyway, Andrew gave me a lift to score some drugs and later that evening we went to his mum's house for a chat and a bit of company. I was still quite hung up about this lad Luke. I know when I spoke about it Andrew seemed really angry that this guy could treat me so badly. I wasn't fully over the affair at that point, and I was very hurt.

Andrew and I started spending more and more time together, but I didn't want anyone knowing because Andrew had a big police investigation going on at the time. Apparently Andy had been running drugs for other guys and the police had pulled him over and found some drugs money, which they confiscated. The other guys didn't believe Andy and threatened to kick the crap out of him. They even stole Andy's car in place of the money and wouldn't leave him alone. I just wanted to keep things quite until things had blown over a bit until the police case was finished with. Andrew was fine and very understanding, but people started to notice once we were seen together on quite a few occasions.

I had been going out with friends quite a lot again. I wanted to get my socialising back to normal, which I knew would also help a great deal when I stopped the gear again. One evening Katie, Lee and I went to a nightclub that held around 1000 people. It was a really well known club, and was packed full of people. The lights were amazing in there and the atmosphere was great. I had a really good night, but yet again I started to feel the worse for wear because I needed to have a smoke of my gear. I had left it at home because I knew it was too risky to do it in the club. Katie had no idea I was still on the gear and I knew she would probably judge me if she knew. Around 4 am we were ready to go home and pass out. On the way home, I wasn't really paying much attention to my speed and was flashed by a camera doing slightly over the limit. I was gutted.

Basically the system here is that there are standard fines for speeding and 3 points are added to your driving licence. Your licence is withdrawn when your penalty points reach 12. The exception to this system is if you have been driving for less than 2 years, in which case your licence is withdrawn at 6 penalty points.

I already had 3 points on my licence when I was caught speeding after I visited Coventry to meet Luke, so I just hoped that I would get the opportunity to do a speed awareness course instead of having 3 more penalty points. The last thing I wanted was to lose my licence. Shortly after, I received a letter with a date for a speed awareness course, which I had to pay for instead of paying the speeding fine. On the day of the course I had problems getting my gear, so I called up to say I wasn't well and I wouldn't be able to make it. The person I spoke to told me that I only had one opportunity to attend. I was so angry that yet again my habit got in the way of an important appointment. As a result I did get the extra 3 penalty points and I had to pay the speeding fine too. Some time later I also found out that my licence had been withdrawn. How stupid could I have been? Instead of paying one fine, I ended up paying two fines and I lost my licence too, so I would now have to re-take my theory and driving tests.

I had decided to start my own business and as Lee was a brilliant DJ I thought it would be a great opportunity for both of us to plan nightclub events. My addiction was still the same, but I still wanted to do something with my life and didn't want to waste any more time. I had heard that the Princes Trust were the people to go to when setting up a business, so I started a course with them and got some idea of what I needed to do to get started in business. Brian had run many businesses over the years and he was a professional with Business Plans. I put a lot of time and effort into my business plan and had to present it to the local Princes Trust board. I asked for a loan of £2000 to help establish my company called Premonition. If ever I needed to know anything I always consulted Brian because he seemed to know something about everything. He doesn't talk about it much, but I know he is highly qualified in engineering and computers. In fact he still works hard and travels all over the world, even at his age. He told me it was quite a big risk with how I wanted to do things, but I really wanted to give it my best shot. Surprisingly my loan application was successful, so I went ahead.

Writing about how you would plan and organise a nightclub event is relatively simple, but doing it in practice is a whole different ball game. I had been to several nightclub events that played the type of music that I wanted, and I had met a lot of DJs and MCs, which helped enormously. The problem arises when you attempt to match available venue dates with the availability of artistes quickly enough to design and print the promotional materials and to arrange for the hire and delivery of supporting equipment such as sound equipment. I also needed to promote this event as much as I possibly could. I even organised transport to and from the venue. At the end of the day I had to put bums on seats and this meant working butt off.

I spent a lot of time promoting my event on the Internet through social networking sites and with ticketing agencies. I also went to other clubbing events and handed out flyers, and I even patrolled the streets distributing flyers and posting them on road signs. I was quite confident that my event would be well supported judging by the positives responses I got from the Internet, and was looking forwards to it immensely. It was my big day and I intended to do it in style. I wanted to look my best so I had my hair specially curled and I wore a small pair of black shorts with gold buttons on the front and a black and white corset, which Brian bought for me. I also had a spray tan the day before and I felt great.

The night of my event started badly. Despite the heavy demand for buses too few people actually turned up to use the buses, so I had to cancel them and pay for them out of my own pocket. This meant a frantic search to find somebody with a car who would give me a lift. When I arrived everything started off just fine, although I was rushed off my feet. I was in and out of the main music room, checking how things looked and then dashing to the main door to attend people paying to get in. I was extremely pleased when I noticed a couple of my friends who were on the gear turned up, including Andrew. The big trouble was that not enough of the people who said they would come, actually did so. In fact less than a quarter turned up so I didn't make enough money. This meant I was in a serious and hugely stressful position. I still owed money for the sound system, and for printing of the flyers, and I still had to pay back the Princes Trust loan. It was a great night, but financially I had blown it, and was now seriously in debt.

ANDREW

Things begun to get a lot more serious with Andrew and I after my event, I was getting to know him for who he really was. Over the years I had either been going out with someone, or I didn't want to be in a relationship after being let down and hurt by Luke. I started spending an awful lot of time with Andrew at his mother's house. I felt like a teenager all over again. I was still using the gear every day and owed quite a bit of money in the process, but that didn't seem to matter. I was just so happy to be with Andrew. I gradually moved my things from my room at Brian's and began to live with Andrew. I felt instantly at home and loved living at Andrew's house with his mother and step father. We found out we had so much in common, and one night Andrew and I lay together on the bed and he turned around and told me he loved me, and I told him that I felt exactly the same. I was so happy.

Our relationship grew stronger as the summer progressed. Gemma and her husband, Marcus would often go camping and leave us alone in the house. This gave us some time alone together, and it was wonderful. We were both content and it was the safest I had felt in a very long time. The next few months were the happiest time for both of us, and we knew we were soul mates from the beginning. We had both been talking about marriage and he asked me would I think about getting engaged to him and I agreed to think about it seriously. A week or two later, it came as a complete shock when Andrew popped the question to me and pulled out a ring from underneath the pillow. I was overwhelmed and gave him a huge hug when he put the ring on my finger. He wasn't sure if it would fit, but it did. The ring has one blue diamond set up high in a clasp and it was just the sort I would have chosen myself. I loved it, and he looked really pleased because he could see I was so happy.

We couldn't wait to tell everyone the news and started to think about what kind of wedding we wanted. Obviously we were dreaming because we just couldn't afford anything lavish. One day at the dinner table, we were talking about what kind of wedding we wanted with Gemma and Marcus, and she asked if we had thought about where we would want the wedding. She said that she knew the perfect venue and church for us, and she reminded Andrew that she had always promised to do all the catering and make the cake for his wedding. She suggested we get married at Guilsborough church with the reception at the village hall. I was a little apprehensive at first because I had always had visions of getting married in a castle somewhere. Perhaps Brian influenced me because his daughter got married in a castle in Italy. Realistically,

I thought we ought to check out her suggestion because it sounded very attractive. Gemma and Marcus said they would also help us financially, and I was hoping my dad would also do the same.

My sister, Karla, was settling back into the real world after her long ordeal in prison and her little boy Cameron was back with her at home. Things were going well for her. She and Liam were getting married and she asked Lucy and me to be her bridesmaids. Lucy, my mum and I went to look at some bridesmaids dresses and to try some on. I was really looking forwards to Karla's wedding because I had only been a bridesmaid once when I was much younger. Lucy and I are different sizes and shapes so we needed to find a style that would suit both of us. We drove to a small but classy shop not far away to look for something suitable. The lady in the shop handed us a few different styles in light blues and a pale lilac colour. The first dress just hung off me but we both liked the second one we tried. Unfortunately that particular style was very expensive and we weren't sure whether the budget would go that far.

Karla then invited us to join her to look for dresses in a place called Hinkley. This was a huge factory outlet that had thousands of dresses that were off the catwalk and only worn once. They were all originally outrageously expensive, but had been substantially reduced. This was a great shop where there were rows and rows of different styles of dresses. Karla had previously wasted a lot of her money by ordering a dress on the Internet, which turned out to be rubbish. Anyway she explained what she was looking for and we tried to help Karla find herself a few dresses. She eventually found a couple that really suited her. Karla was quite laid back about the whole situation, while we were telling her how lovely she looked. She made her decision so that just left Lucy and me. We tried several dresses on but nothing seemed right. I felt that Karla was getting stressed as we rummaged around. The trouble was that Lucy and I loved the first dress that we had seen at the previous shop. In the end Karla put a deposit down on her dress and we left.

The following weekend we went shopping in Milton Keynes and once again Lucy and I were not impressed, but we could see that Karla just wanted us to pick something and go home, so we had to make a rushed decision. In my eyes they didn't have the 'Wow factor'. Later that evening I got a message from Lucy to say that she didn't like her dress and was worried about having to tell Karla. I told Lucy that I felt the same. We knew it was Karla's big day, but we still needed to feel comfortable on the day too. Karla didn't take the news too well, because it meant yet another shopping trip. Lucy had previously seen a dress at another shop that she wanted to show me in her favourite colour, turquoise. It was a silky satin style, with no straps. I wasn't completely sure at first, but once we both tried them on, they looked great.

The day of Karla's wedding arrived, and I went to meet Lucy and my mum at the hairdressers. I decided on having my hair done to the side in curls and pinned up, it looked stunning and boosted my self-esteem. I actually felt like a bridesmaid. It was the first time my sister had really met Andy who was in one of his joking moods and made Lucy laugh. Andy wore a cream suit, which made him stand out. It was a great occasion for Andy to meet people and for them to meet him. It felt great to be at a family event with a man to hold onto, because previously I was always the one without a partner. Andrew also offered to sing on my sister's big day, which I felt was a great present from both of us.

Andy and I bought enough heroin to last us, while we out for the day. I had all my things with me to get ready at the hotel where Karla was getting married. My first impression was that the place was too small, but once we walked in, it was actually quite nice. I was extremely nervous about having to walk in front of everyone, because I felt I was on show. The whole event was beautiful, and fortunately it was a gorgeous, hot summer day too.

After the speeches and toasts, Andy went and set his sound equipment up to perform his songs. Everyone stared at him in disbelief, and afterwards he had an awful lot of people coming up to him saying how good he was. As we were the newly engaged couple, we also had our photos taken. We went to many nice occasions with each other over the next couple of months. We also went to a few 'gigs' that Andrew had been booked for in different places like; singing at weddings and pubs.

It was generous of Gemma and Marcus to let us live in their house, and I loved living there but we needed our own privacy and to start a life together, so I decided to look for an apartment with the Housing Association. Andrew and I had been on and off heroin in the first few months of being together, but it wasn't long before we ourselves stabilised and back on track with a methadone programme. On one particular day I saw one advertised in our town and put in a bid for it. A week later Andrew and I were having a meal with his Nan, his real dad, and his wife Jane, when I got a call from my dad telling me there was a message for me on his answering machine from the Housing Association. They said that we had five days to view the flat and decide if we wanted it. Andrew and I were so pleased that we jumped around cuddling each other. It was the best birthday present ever for Andrew.

Andrew and I were lying in bed one night when I heard a loud bang. I didn't take much notice at the time, and it wasn't until we both heard another explosion that Andy's mum came rushing out of her room screaming that the van was on fire. We jumped up immediately and rushed downstairs. Andy tried to find the front door keys quickly before the car blew up and set the house on fire with it. We were all rushing around like headless chickens, until finally he got outside and used the garden hose to get the fire under control. Meanwhile Gemma called the Fire Service. I don't think any of us could believe what had just happened. The van was brand new when Andy had bought it a year ago. The Fire Service turned up, but they didn't have much to do because Andy had already put the fire out. They also couldn't understand how the fire had started, but we found out later that it was an electrical fault. Losing your car is like having your legs cut off.

A couple of days later I woke up feeling very poorly, but as the day went on it got progressively worse; as if I had flu. My chest hurt and I had a severe pain in my lower rib cage. Andy could see I was getting worse and offered to take me to hospital. On the way to hospital I got even worse and began to panic because I felt like passing out with the pain. When we arrived at the hospital I struggled to even get out of the car. I couldn't breath properly at this stage and was taking small breaths, so I had difficulty telling the doctor what the problem was. The doctor told me that I needed to have a chest X-ray. I had no idea what was wrong with me and was so stressed that I burst into tears. Andy held my hand and looked extremely worried as well. I just lay there in agonising pain. I had never experienced pain like it. After the X-ray I had to have a blood test and I knew this would be a problem. I had no veins, due to my heroin misuse over the years. The nurse couldn't find a vein so the doctor tried, and succeeded. Whenever I am in trouble I always reach out for my mum. I felt like a small child feeling completely helpless and wanting her mum. My mum finally came and she was very quite, but obviously worried and sat with me until my results came through. The doctor finally came back and told us that I was suffering from mild pneumonia. He advised me to rest, and prescribed a course of strong antibiotics. I was so relieved that I didn't have something else seriously wrong with me.

About two weeks after Andy's van burnt out he began looking for a new car. He found an advertisement in the Auto Trader, so he and Marcus went to have a look. Later that day he came back with it. It was a lovely Audi with leather interior. Andy looked a lot happier because lately things had been tough on him, and I could also see his illness (bipolar) taking its toll. He wasn't very good at coping and anything that created more stress for him also caused his illness to get worse. It was something that I wished I could change and help him with, but it was one of those things that we both have to live with. Despite the problems we have been lucky to have support from Gemma and Marcus in many ways.

It wasn't long after Andy's birthday that we went to view the flat and we were pleased to see it was a really lovely place and in good condition. It had laminated flooring throughout and was decorated in modern wallpaper. There was nothing we needed to do to it apart from move our things in. My friend Brian helped me with the rental deposit, and then my dad helped to move my things in. Gemma and Marcus helped us with getting a settee and a few other things, and later a washing machine as the one we had was really old.

A few days before we moved in permanently to our new home I sat on the bed waiting for Andy to come home. I heard him pull up on the drive and then there was such a commotion, so I went to see what all the fuss was about. Andy had brought home a tiny little Staffordshire Bullterrier curled up in a ball in a large dog bed. I was so happy. Andy had bought the best present ever for me. I had always wanted a puppy and had been talking about it for some time, but didn't think Andy would actually get me one. As we sat chatting, the little pup opened his eyes and instantly began to explore his new territory, and I could tell he was a clever little thing. We decide to name him Spike.

Now that we were settled in, I began to think about our wedding plans again. My dad had told me he wanted to speak to me, because he realised that we were deadly serious about getting married in the summer of 2011. He had helped by paying towards my two other sisters' weddings, so he told me he would do the same for me. I was over the moon about this, and knew that with the help of both families we could really have a gorgeous wedding now that we knew what sort of money we were looking at spending and what the budget was. If anyone had told me this would be happening three years ago, when I was in the depths of despair in prison, I would not have believed it.

MY WEDDING

The immediate task was to view the church and hall
in Guilsborough to be sure that it would be suitable.
Gemma was full of suggestions and good ideas,
between us we would make the wedding what it was.
The church itself was beautiful and the hall down the
quiet village road had a lovely feel to it. There was a
kitchen on one side, which had mostly everything
Gemma would need for serving the food with her
army of helpers. The organisation was brilliant. How
she managed to do this as well as everything else, I
will never know. We made the decision there and
then that this was the right venue. It was perfect in
every way.

Now I could start doing what every other bride does: start buying lots of nice things for the reception, the church and obviously the most important thing, the dress. I wanted a butterfly theme, and I had seen a dress that I had fell in love with on a website, but I knew it was going to be hugely expensive, so I was hoping to find one similar but for less money. I decided to ask both my sisters to be bridesmaids, and Andy wanted the two children of his friend to be flower girls. In effect I had four bridesmaids, and my brother as an usher. Andy's Nan used to be a seamstress so she would do any alterations to the dresses if they were needed. She is so creative and artistic, and she said she would make our homemade invitations, which would keep the cost down. I also asked Andy's Nan if she could make me a name board with the seating arrangements, which she also did in a butterfly theme. Gemma and her husband had taken so much on their shoulders. Gemma kept a list of things including the wedding folder to keep track of everything. Apart from making our wedding cake she also organised all the food and drink, found lots of helpers from work, made our order of service books and our beautiful table cloths. When I think about it, she and her husband Marcus did an awful lot for our wedding. Marcus also made sure he knew where everyone would be so he could drive everyone by mini bus. I know I couldn't of done it without them both. My friend Brian can do calligraphy, so he wrote all the names on the butterflies to place on edges of the wine glasses and also on the name board. When I think back, it seems as though all the elderly people I know, such as my Nan, Andy's Nan and my friend Brian, are all so talented. They must have been educated in their generation in a way that we no longer do. I was very fortunate to have such talented people all helping with many of the important and expensive parts of wedding decor, this brought the cost down quite a bit, but gave it that extra wow factor.

I wanted my day to be a dream wedding, as you only plan on doing it once and you want that day to be perfect. I worried about being on methadone as I wanted to be completely back to normal without having to rely on any medication. I wanted to enjoy every minute of it without feeling poorly at any point so we both decided to take a little more methadone on that day. I couldn't afford to take any risks. Previously I had resolved to get myself clean in plenty of time so I would be off all opiates for that day, but I was deluding myself as usual. This isn't something that you can do quickly, and so I would be struggling to get clean in time.

After a long chat with Mark, the vicar of the church, we agreed on 9th July 2011 as the date of the wedding. This meant I could begin to send out invitations, book things that we would need such as transport. A horse and carriage would have been nice, but they were too expensive so we settled on an all-day limousine. Andy and I were so happy because the wedding arrangements had started to roll.

Andrew had been feeling unwell with the same symptoms that I had with pneumonia. He had been to the doctors on a few different occasions but the doctor just gave him some antibiotics and anti-inflammatory tablets. Nothing seemed to work and he continued to suffer. I was quite worried because of the wedding coming up and because his illness had gone on for so long. We were invited to a camping trip with Gemma and Marcus in Great Yarmouth. We all knew Andrew was still not well, but he wanted to go, and just have a break. We had quite an early night the first day. Spike was in his element. He could play with his toys, and run around freely. Just being out in the open air always kept him amused. We went into Yarmouth and looked around the shops on our second day. The next day it was sunny and bright, and we went on a leisurely boat trip. Andrew's health declined rapidly, so we made the decision to go home the next morning.

We made our way with Marcus and Gemma to meet my dad and my brother at a small specialist shop to get suits for all the boys. The tailor took me straight over to a lightweight pale grey suit that would be ideal for the summer. I was just hoping our day would be sunny. Once Andrew had the full outfit on, with the waistcoat, shirt and tie, I couldn't believe how hansom he looked. My dad, Marcus and my brother also looked great.

The boys were done, and by chance we noticed a gorgeous, grape coloured bridesmaid dress in another shop opposite the tailors, so Gemma and I made a mad dash to have a look. It was so exciting. I nearly fainted when I saw they had three of them in the right sizes, I just needed to know that my sisters wouldn't mind me getting them without them being there. I also noticed that they were a discontinued designer brand and were extremely reasonably priced. I called my sisters to check and they said that I should get them. I had done well in a single day.

The following week Gemma and I planned to go to Hinkley to the warehouse to try some dresses. My mum had the day off and came as well. This was the first time my mum and Gemma got to meet each other. Once we arrived at the shop I started to hunt for my dream dress. An assistant asked me what kind of style and size I was looking for, and selected some dresses for me to try on. One of them was just what I was looking for. I came out of the dressing room to show my mum and Gemma, and they looked at me in amazement. I looked in a mirror and couldn't believe how lovely this dress was. The assistant rushed over to get me a matching veil and a tiara. The overall effect was outstanding. I intended to look stunning and in this dress I would go one better. Everything had so far fallen into place, and I felt like a very lucky girl.

I noticed one of the clasps on my ring was bent and I showed it to Gemma, and she said she would get it fixed. My ring had originally came from Hatton Garden and had been hand made with a special blue diamond. Andrew's real dad was a jeweller at one time and had bulk purchased it in a group of other rings. Andrew and I then went shopping for our wedding rings. Surprisingly we found exactly what we wanted in the jewellery section of a well-known store. I knew the gold would match my gorgeous engagement ring. The following day Gemma returned with my engagement ring. I was so pleased to see what they had done, and it was such a great present from Gemma and Marcus. They had put in a whole new clasp and had polished and re-set the diamond. It looked like a new ring and I was thrilled with the outcome. I also needed some jewellery. On the Internet I found a choker style necklace with three rows of pearls with a diamante butterfly in the middle and a pair of butterfly earrings with pearls and diamantes and a matching bracelet. It was stunning and I knew it would all match beautifully with my dress and the theme of the wedding. My friend Brian ordered it for me as a wedding present. Could there be a better friend?

Now I needed a photographer. Fortunately my neighbour mentioned one that she had used. I looked at his beautifully presented work and I knew he was definitely the one for the job. Andrew and I had decided on a local guy for the disco because he had a very good set up for the stage. I also asked him if he could set up some up lights around the hall to give the hall some colour.

There were so many things to plan for a wedding that I was afraid something might go wrong, so I carefully ticked everything off my list as I went along. My big day was going to be a battle between my determination and my fragility. Any small knock-back from anything that didn't go to plan could upset me and reduce me to tears, or even destroy my whole day. These thoughts hounded me everyday. Thank goodness there were only a few things that needed doing now. I was so worried that something wouldn't turn out like I wanted it to, but I think any bride would have felt the same. Gemma and Marcus also booked us into a really nice hotel for two evenings because we couldn't afford an expensive honeymoon to some remote part of the world. The hotel had a swimming pool, and spa treatment, so at least I would have a touch of luxury.

The day before the wedding we needed to go to the hall to get it ready for the following day. Gemma and Marcus had arrived there early with their very good friends Julia and Malcolm. Julia and Malcolm had come to help us organise everything and worked like proverbial slaves. Gemma was were there preparing the kitchen and making sure there were plenty of plates and cutlery. She also dressed one side of the hall. Out of all of us, she had one of the most difficult jobs, and she was also under the most pressure because she was doing all of the catering. I was dashing around like a scalded cat fixing chair covers, blowing up balloons, putting up drapes, arranging table covers and mirrors and candlesticks along with Andrew on one side of the hall, while Gemma worked hard on the opposite side. The list was never ending. Outside the entrance there was a gazebo with two olive trees either side dressed with bows and butterflies. Julia and Malcolm kindly leant it to us and decorated it the following morning. They gave it the extra wow factor. We also borrowed a huge easel and the butterfly name board was placed on it at the entrance so everyone knew where they were sitting. By the time we all finished the place looked spectacular: just how I had imagined it to be in my head.

Andrew and I had stayed at the flat the night before which I knew was supposed to be unlucky, but we wanted to have a stress free evening before hand. Andrew went to his mum's house at 7 am, as he needed to get ready with Marcus, who was best man. I was picked up by my mum to go to the hairdressers in the next town, where we met up with the little flower girls and my sister, Lucy.

It took just over an hour for all of us to have our hair done and then get back to my mum's house, where we all went to get dressed up. I was so excited. I hadn't felt like this in a long, long time. Opiates are supposed to depress your emotions and feelings, but that morning I certainly didn't feel like that. I had all the natural feelings of a bride to be; butterflies in my stomach and an excited buzz. Perhaps my emotions were running so high, even methadone couldn't stop them. The house was like a mad house with all of us dashing about in all directions. Jason, the photographer, arrived with his assistant to take some extra snaps, so I was really happy about that. I didn't want a moment to be missed on such an important day. The photographers began taking pictures of absolutely everything that was happening as we dressed. I wanted the pictures to tell a story of the whole day. Then the florist arrived with my bouquet and the other flowers. They were so beautiful I could have cried and I gave the florist the biggest cuddle to say thank you.

Lucy helped lace me into my dress while the photographer took a few pictures, and when I finally looked in the mirror, I couldn't believe the reflection was really me. I felt like a princess, like I always imagined it. Before I knew it the limousine arrived. I was finally having something good in my life and it felt like a dream. My dad didn't really say much when he saw me, but I could tell he thought I looked lovely. As we drove away, all the neighbours waved us off, which reminded me of when I was in the carnival and people waved as we paraded down the streets.

When we pulled up at the church I could still see people walking inside. I looked around and saw my little puppy, Spike, with Andrew's dad who brought him over to me to fuss a little. I then looked at my sister, and I just couldn't control how I was feeling as the tears rolled down my face, I was thinking about what a tough year it had been and how it had all been transformed. It was such an overwhelming emotional experience that I just wanted it to go on and on. I didn't want it to end. The moment had come where I had to get out of the car and walk up the aisle with my dad.

Andy and I decided that rather than traditional organ music on my entrance, we would have some really touching music for the ceremony and traditional organ music for us to walk out to.. We chose two songs that meant a lot to us. The music began and as dad and I slowly walked in I felt the tears welling up. I had only just composed myself outside, but now I had no chance of controlling how I was feeling, so out came the tears. I looked straight up the aisle where I could see Andrew looking back at me. We both had a tearful moment once we set eyes on each other. I was a nervous wreck.

I was so nervous I could barely get my words out during the ceremony. I even made a mistake with Andrew's name, and everyone laughed. We saw the funny side too, and this actually snapped me out of my nervousness. At least the hard part was over and I took a huge breath of relief as we both went to sign the register. I could see that Andrew was really struggling, as he was still unwell, but he was determined to make the day as special as possible for me and everyone else. I couldn't stop smiling as we left the church to traditional organ music. As we stepped out of the church, hand in hand, the sun came out as though a light had just been switched on. Could I have planned it any better? It was miraculous.

Everyone was outside for the usual photos, and then Andrew and I got into the limousine for the short drive to the reception hall. We both had time at this point to reflect on how the day had been so far. It was a dream wedding and we felt so fortunate considering our personal circumstances. We couldn't stop talking about how fortunate and lucky we were to have parents that did what they did for us. The hall was full of people and I began talking excitedly to everyone before the meal. Everything ran like clock work: just as I imagined it would. After the meal the chocolate fountain lady arrived to set it up. This went down like a storm, particularly with the children.

The disco entertainer asked us if we wanted to do our first dance, so we took to the floor. As the music played, Andrew and I just held one another as everyone watched. It was so romantic and amazingly it was something we had never done before. Later we cut the cake, accompanied by more photos. Afterwards I noticed Andrew sitting down, because he was so exhausted and was ready to leave. I think my dad wasn't too pleased that we were going to leave in the next hour, but Andrew's mum could also see that he was suffering and told him we were going whether he liked it or not.

I knew I had been very fortunate that my mother in law and father in law had done such a grand job with everything, but most of all the food. All of their friends that had helped, had also done us more than proud. I could never thank them enough for making our wedding day what it was.

Everyone waved us off, and that was our wedding day all finished. It had taken a huge amount of time and effort to organise, and in the blink of an eye it was all over, but it was truly all worth it. We were dropped off at the hotel where we fell on top of the bed. We were both so tired, but we both felt it had been an amazing day for both of us. Any normal newly married couple would probably have been intimate after getting married, but all we could do was collapse with exhaustion. It had been such a very long day for us both.

On our way home the following day we took a detour to ask my friend Brian what he thought of the wedding. I was surprised to hear that all our guests had stayed on dancing the night away until gone midnight, which was exactly what I wanted to hear. Gemma told me later that everyone had said it was the best wedding they had ever been to, and how much they had enjoyed it. I was so pleased.

SINGING

Not long after the wedding Andrew's health spiralled downwards. I sat up with Andrew most of the night because he was having serious pains; very much like I had when I had pneumonia. By the morning he was in agony so I called an ambulance. It them around ten minutes to arrive and I told them he was on methadone and that he also had bipolar. They gave him a shot of morphine but it didn't do a thing to help. He had to have a number of shots before it took some of the pain off. Andrew agreed to go to hospital so that they could check to find out what the real problem was. I drove to the hospital with Spike in the car and I began to cry, I was so worried. I knew Andy was seriously ill, because he wouldn't make a fuss about anything like that. He was extremely strong when it came to illness. The doctors gave Andrew a series of tests, and then he was put on an antibiotic drip before he was told he also had pneumonia. Gemma told me that she would bring Andrew home. I was a little dubious about leaving him, but I couldn't leave little Spike for to long on his own. So I drove home so I could feed Spike and to have some methadone as I felt I needed it. I hadn't had anything all day. When Andrew arrived home a couple of hours later he told me that he had pneumonia all that time, including the day of our wedding. Fortunately, after taking a course of tablets and plenty of rest Andrew began to get better.

I was quite lost after all the planning and excitement leading up of our wedding. I hadn't got so much to think about, apart from moving forwards now that we were married. Everyday seemed quite dull after the wedding, not because we were unhappy with each other, but because we wanted life to change in a dramatic way. We knew that coming off methadone wouldn't be easy. Two addicts together is a lot harder than one, so we knew we would have to stay strong for one another.

Andrew's bipolar was also very up and down, and we visited the doctor to look at changing his medication. He was given a new prescription to try, and for the next couple of weeks I noticed an improvement in his mood and his behaviour. Like me, every time something came along that made life difficult he couldn't cope and he became depressed, only much, much worse. More than anything I just wanted to help him through his difficult ups and downs. I know this is an illness he will always have, but when you love somebody you stick by them, through thick and thin.

Andrew had been working on his car, and the following day we had just been to collect our scripts from our counselling session, when I turned the stereo on. It wasn't working properly and we started to argue, because he said I didn't know what I was doing and attempted to do it himself. Before we realised, we ran into the back of the car in front. The whole front end of our car was smashed up. It was such a stupid argument and to this day I don't know why we didn't just wait until we could pull over. Andrew began to shout at me more, because he blamed me for causing him to lose his concentration. It was a horrible and frightening situation.

I wanted to get my own car back on the road and I mentioned it to my dad, who arranged for a few things to be fixed so that I could get it booked in for the MOT test as I still had a thousand pounds left from my wedding money. I had to wait a couple of weeks before I could get all the work done and booked in at a local garage.

Andrew was worried about whether his voice would be affected from having pneumonia, so he decided to have a practice at his mum's house where all his singing equipment was kept. I dropped him off one afternoon and told him to call me once he had finished. I had been on the Internet and seen several singing competitions were taking place, so I entered Andrew. He was good enough and I knew he could do really well. The first competition was called 'The Voice' starting in 2012. The second one was 'Britain's Got Talent'. Later that evening I told Andrew what I had done, and he said that his voice needed some work, but he thought it was a good idea.

One evening I asked my friend Brian to give me a lift to an appointment in the next town. It was rush hour and really busy on the way back, and as we came up to a round about and a car pulled out on us, so Brian slammed on his brakes. We didn't hit the car, but within seconds we were hit, from behind by a bus, and I flew forwards hitting my head and straining my neck. It was all so sudden. Brian calmly got out and sorted out the insurance details with the bus driver. Brian said he felt fine but my neck hurt, so I reported a whiplash injury and put in an insurance claim.

A couple of weeks after my car was fixed I took it to the garage for an MOT certificate. I prayed that it would pass as there was no way I could afford to get any more work done on it. Later that evening when I picked it up, they told me it had passed. That night I went to my dad's house to get my insurance. I was really pleased to hear my dad was going to pay for my insurance for a whole year, because I wasn't completely sure what way things would go once I got round to his house. He can change his mind just like that unfortunately, even if it was left over wedding money. He can be very unpredictable at times. I don't think my dad trusted me with the money. He decided he didn't want to insure my car with his credit card in case they tried to take it the following year, so I called my friend Brian. He said it would be fine to transfer the money to his account and he would arrange the insurance on-line. I was so pleased that my little car was all sorted and roadworthy. This was just what Andrew and I needed. It had been a real pain without a car since our crash. The weather had got terribly cold and walking everywhere was a nightmare.

Andrew had been searching for a new car as his dad had said we could either have some money towards a honeymoon or towards a car. I think Andrew was desperate to get another car again, so he began searching for another Audi and found one on a website that sounded perfect. So Andrew organised to get a lift to Sheffield with my old friend Paul to view the car. I knew that he would return with this particular one, and later that evening he did.

I was checking my e-mails when noticed that I there was one from 'The Voice' saying that Andrew had been booked for an audition the following weekend in London. This wasn't really enough time, but we both thought it would be a great opportunity for him and also a nice day out to look around London. I could feel Andrew becoming a little nervous as we approached Earls Court where Andrew would be doing his audition. One of the annoying rules was that he could not wait with friends or family members while waiting to sing. I know he needed my support and encouragement, but this wasn't going to be the case unfortunately. I would have to wait patiently and slightly worried that things wouldn't go his way. We decided to have a drink in a pub not very far from where the audition was. The pub had a really London feel to it; lots of people sat talking and getting on with their daily lives. I had a wine, while the men drank beer and Gemma had an orange juice. I'm always amazed at how expensive things are in London compared to back home. At this point I really thought Andrew had a very good chance. At last Andrew finally got to the front and off he went. He didn't say much, which I took as a sign that his nerves were beginning to show quite dramatically.

While we waited for Andrew we walked around the streets. London had its Christmas face on and looked fantastic, with Christmas trees and lots of lights that looked like icicles and huge baubles hanging from the ceilings. Having the time to walk around London and look at all the intriguing things was a great day out in itself, but it also turned out to be a very long day. I was also wondering how Andrew was doing and I kept on checking my watch as the time was ticking by. In the end we decided to go back and check how things were going. We walked into the reception area and I found a couple of seats and sat down with Marcus and Gemma. I began talking to another girl who was also waiting for her boyfriend. She couldn't sit still for a minute. I thought I was a little nervous, but she was on a different level of nervousness altogether.

Suddenly I saw Andrew on his way down, so I jumped up to see what had happened, and he just said that they didn't put him through to the next round. I didn't know what to say because I had such high hopes for him. He told us that when his group had been called through, he was the first one to start, which made him feel extremely tense. After he sang his piece, the next guy had an amazing voice and blew the competition away. Andrew said that he hadn't heard somebody as good as him in a long time. I could tell by his face that this had really affected him a big way, and I was beginning to think it was a bad idea entering him for this competition. I didn't think it would upset him quite so much as it did. Then he went on to say that it was a waste of time because his voice wasn't good enough anymore. All I could do was try to reassure him and snap him out of this depressive frame of mind.

Later on when we arrived back home we sat and talked about how the day had been. Andrew admitted that he had messed up; he didn't breathe in the right places, and he hadn't practiced enough. All the waiting before the audition hadn't helped as he had to sit around for hours with nobody to speak to. So that was the first audition out of the window.

Andrew woke up the next day, and thought about things a lot more logically. I was on the laptop at home checking my e-mails when I noticed that I had another message from a different competition, 'Britain's Got Talent'. I turned straight round to Andrew and told him that he had another audition to go to if he wanted. He had two weeks to get his voice back in condition, so he agreed. The two weeks flew by and then we needed to attend the audition at the NEC in Birmingham. On this occasion we thought we would do things slightly differently: we went alone. I drove and Andrew tried to relax. I couldn't believe how big the NEC was, as I had never been there before. We parked as far away as possible so Andrew could have one last practice.

We only had ten minutes left at this stage to walk up to the queue, where we stood waiting for around 20 minutes before it started to rain. Fortunately we just managed to get under cover. Finally we got inside and were allocated a number. I took a seat while Andrew grabbed us a sandwich to share. I was watching some kids doing back flips and break dancers practicing a routine and I could see a large camera filming people. We found a seat in the right audition area and waited to hear what we needed to do next. A lady came out and spoke to everyone over a microphone. She explained that they were running late, but we would all get seen soon. We went out for a cigarette a couple of times as the waiting seemed to go on and on, but after a few hours Andrew's group was called. We followed everyone upstairs to where we had to sit and wait yet again, but this time, we were only waited ten minutes. Andrew's name was called and he walked into the audition. I gave him a kiss and wished him good luck. I went up to the door and put my ear close to see if I could hear him, but I only caught a small snippet at the end. He came out and looked quite serious, but pleased at the same time. He told me that it went well, but nobody would know the results until February.

LIVING WITH BIPOLAR

Andrew was diagnosed with Bipolar Disorder when he was a lot younger and a year ago he had to attend a medical assessment to see if he was unfit to work. Andrew was classed in the highest tier for his illness, so it meant he was a danger to himself, and meant he could claim extra benefits. Now that we are married we claim social security benefits as a couple. For the last year there has been no change in his illness. Day to day it can get worse or slightly better, but it will never go away, unfortunately. He had to go for another medical assessment just before Christmas and he was completely honest about how his illness can affect his everyday life. Recently we were informed that he is no longer eligible for this kind of benefit. Naturally we are appealing against the assessment. It appears that if you appeal, both our Employment and Support Allowances would be stopped, including our housing benefit, pending the outcome of the appeal. I was infuriated by this stupid procedure because in the meantime we needed something to live on. It took weeks of frustrating negotiation to get our basic welfare payments reinstated, and even now it has not been fully resolved.

I know that we are very lucky to get welfare support, but it doesn't excuse the fact that the system is so badly organised that it can leave people without any benefit, when they so clearly need it. I know that in other countries we wouldn't be treated so well and I am grateful that I live in a country that tries to take care of the less fortunate.

I have spoken to Andrew about children before, but this isn't something I would ever entertain until we have both been off drugs for a long time. I could never put another human being through the things I have suffered. When children are born to addicts, they have to go through the agony of a detox. How could anyone put their own child through all that pain? I certainly couldn't. Having children is supposed to be an amazing moment: not a moment of guilt and worry.

I often think about what I would be like if I had never become an addict. What would I be doing? Where would I be? I can't say, and I can't even guess if I would be any happier than I am now. There is no way that we can know such things. I think I've made lots of mistakes over the years, but that is all in the past. The only thing I can change is the future ahead of me. My past is going to make life more difficult and limit my opportunities, so the future is not going to be easy. At least I have the support of three very important people in my life; my husband, my little Spike and my best friend Brian.

We had been invited to Nan and Granddad's 60th wedding anniversary and we wanted to make an effort for his family, even though we didn't feel up to it. We sat and chatted for about an hour before dinner and I could see that Andrew was becoming more and more pale. He turned to me and said that he wanted to go because he felt so ill, but we stayed on until the food was served. Andrew didn't eat at all because he felt so bad and his moods were up and down.

I could see in Andrew's face that everything had piled on top of him. We had so many worries to cope with; our welfare money had stopped, we had letters through the door all the time for different debts, and the rent for the flat was over due. Andrew's illness had been really bad lately. He was so depressed that he was finding it difficult to cope with anything. Andrew decided he wanted to go home once everyone had eaten. His Nan and granddad decided they would go home too so we offered them a lift. I felt like I was at rock bottom. It had been a terrible week, so I turned around and told Andrew that I would come back later as I needed to get it all off my chest.

I went straight around to my friend's house and burst into tears. I told him how upset I was and how I felt that life was starting to wear me down again. I should be on a high still; just married, with a lovely flat, and a lovely little dog, which we love dearly. On the other hand, how can I be happy when I have got all of the other things dragging me down? I sat on Brian's leather sofa, pouring my heart out. When I thought about it, I hadn't cried so much as I had in the last year, as there had been a lot of problems for us to cope with. Brian said that I had always been such a happy person, despite my lifestyle, but he had to admit that he had never seen me cry so much as I had in the past year.

I explained to him that things would get better once we were off our medication and clean. I know that our habit is a big part in making us unhappy and causing Andrew's illness to worsen. After breaking down and sharing exactly how things were making me feel, I began to calm down. It made me so much better getting it all off of my chest, but after the day I had just experienced. I left shortly after speaking to Brian and went to collect Andrew. He had calmed down and told me he was sorry for shouting at me. I told him that I didn't deserve any of that and I could tell by his face he felt a little guilty. When you love somebody you will put up with your partner's faults and problems, because they become your own as well as theirs.

I've been having different thoughts about what I want to do as a career. My friend Brian said he thinks I would make a brilliant PA for somebody, and he is probably right because I'm quite efficient when I need to get things done. I've also had a long time ambition to be a Physiotherapist or something like that. I'm great with people and I have already learnt something about bones and muscles when I was in prison. I hope that I can still claim welfare benefits while I'm studying, otherwise it will make life very difficult.

Recently my friend Brian wanted to take a picture of me for the front cover of his latest novel, which is set in the 1900s. He even named the principal character after me. The picture he took was great, but he had to do a lot of photographic trickery to make it look old and grainy. He took the photo in a local hotel, so it would have an Edwardian feel to it. I wore a dress with the pearl choker I wore for my wedding and a scarf over my shoulders, as women in those days didn't show a lot of flesh. I can tell you that it feels good to be on the front of a book. Brian also took the fabulous front cover photo for this book, and kindly proof read the original manuscript. I may be an on-off heroin addict, but I am still doing things in life that most people wouldn't.

I live in hope that life will change now in a much more positive way, so Andrew, Spike and I can have a good future and a less stressful time. Life is full of many ups and downs, but it's finding a way to cope with it, and that's exactly what I need to do. I need to learn to cope when the going gets tough.

Since I have been with Andrew, his family have been a great support in many ways. They have supported us through all of the terrible problems we have had to go through over the last year. We feel we are very lucky to have the love and support from them both.

CONCLUSION

It is important to remember that heroin addiction is an illness and needs to be treated accordingly. It is an illness that has no cure. The best that sufferers can hope for is to control the addiction with will power and medication and recovery over a period of time. It is an illness like many others, having the need to use heroin to reduce the pain. Anyone in discomfort and serious pain reaches out for medication. You become depended quickly, and your tolerance increases the more you use. This in turn results in a bigger habit.

If you have a partner, a family member or a friend who is an addict and you are trying to help them, or just trying to cope with it, then ignorance and stupidity are your worse enemies. Find out all you can and know the risks. You won't be affected unless you let it happen. The best defence against addiction and dependency is knowledge. Know and understand what you are up against. Never become curious or intrigued, because it only takes a few times of using and you will also become hooked. From that point on it is only a matter of time before you become infected with full-blown heroin addiction. Once you have the illness you will be relentlessly pursued to keep taking more heroin to avoid the intense pain of withdrawal.

Such is the pain, that you will go to any lengths to avoid it. There is nothing you will not do to relieve the pain. There are no limits to the depths you will sink to in order to sustain your habit. Unlike other illnesses, recovery is infinitely more painful than the illness itself, so it requires considerable courage to even contemplate volunteering for the recovery process. My advice is to avoid heroin like the plague.

Addicts who come off opiate medication slowly over a long period are more likely to succeed in the long term. Rushing into a detox programme can result in failure. It isn't an easy addiction to overcome and it takes many years to return back to normal physical and mental health.

My purpose in writing this book was to give you, and all parents an honest insight into the world of a heroin addict and the daily problems they face. It is a sad but genuine account of my life, and a sober warning to others. During the course of writing this account I have learnt much about myself, and my addiction. I would dearly love to end this book and claim that I was cured, but heroin addiction isn't like that. However, I do recognise what I need to do to reach this goal. My first step is to take one day at a time and keep strong. Hopefully my life will improve with time once I am off all opiates. I know that this must be followed immediately by the support of blocker medication (Naltrexone), because I don't have the will power to resist slip-ups: no heroin addict does. I know that I am easy prey to life's little knocks, so I need help to conquer this weakness. I am impetuous and impatient so I need to control myself better. At least I am being honest instead of deluding myself. I also know that I will probably rely on this medication for many years to come. In the meantime I have to disassociate myself from any friends who are still users. This is going to be very difficult, but I recognise that 'friends' have been the primary reason for my past slip-ups. I would be foolish to make any promises to never use again. This isn't something that I can definitely say I will never do unfortunately, but it is something that I can hope for.

Wish me luck.

ABOUT THE AUTHOR

Marie Maloney lives in rural England with her husband and her dog, Spike. From her early childhood she has had a passionate interest in riding horses, which continues to this day. She writes in her spare time to support her campaign for reforming the way drugs offenders are treated and rehabilitated. She brought the plight of under-age drug abuse to the attention of the public through TV appearances, resulting in a change to the law. She also has passionate views about reforming the way the law currently treats drug offenders because the current system is clearly ineffective. She wants to improve the way that children in schools are made aware of the dangers of drugs and alcohol abuse, because the existing methods are not working, otherwise we would have fewer drugs offenders in prisons. She has also written a Wedding Handbook based on her own experiences.

Printed in Great Britain
by Amazon